THE POSTCONCILIAR CHRISTIAN

THE POSTCONCILIAR CHRISTIAN

the meaning of
the priesthood of the laity

TIMOTHY McCARTHY, O.P.

foreword by
DOROTHY DAY

P. J. KENEDY & SONS   NEW YORK

Imprimi potest: Gilbert J. Graham, O.P.
              Prior Provincial

Nihil obstat: Kevin D. O'Rourke, O.P.
              John V. Thomas, O.P.
              Censores deputati

Imprimatur: James J. Byrne, S.T.D.
              Archbishop of Dubuque

Dubuque, Iowa, January 26, 1967

The nihil obstat *and* imprimatur *are official declarations that a book or pamphlet is free of doctrinal or moral error. No implication is contained therein that those who have granted the* nihil obstat *and* imprimatur *agree with the contents, opinions, or statements expressed.*

for my family and friends

FOREWORD

The original title of this book is "The Priesthood of the Laity," a concept that has always fascinated me even from childhood— and *The Postconciliar Christian* has clarified for me the reason why. And that is, man's need to worship. The author himself says, "One can find here a solid and clear exposition of what it means when someone shares in Christ's royal and prophetical priesthood." And he feels satisfied that he has said what he wanted to say, in a writing that is most important for our time.

We hear a great deal of talk about the apostolate of the laity, but little about the priesthood of the laity. Father McCarthy makes the distinction very clear between priest and people, but he points the similarities, too, in the role of priest and victim, one who sacrifices and one who is sacrificed.

Thank God the laymen are now participating actively in worship, joining with the priest in dialogue around the altar, offering a sacrifice for God's honor and glory, in thanksgiving, in penance, and in supplication. It is coming easier to the laity, and to the priest to take it from the laity, this sharing of his priesthood which he has so long considered his own prerogative. To illustrate what I mean let me give one or two incidents.

There was a dear old woman who used to visit us at our farm in Easton, Pennsylvania, our first venture in a community on the land where the chapel in the barn was central in that our life was built around it. Our most honored guests were the young priests who came to spend their vacations with us and to share with us their own fresh enthusiasm. Seminarians came, too; and one night one of these, seeing the elderly woman acting in her role as mother and grandmother, making the sign of the cross over the children before they went to bed, challenged her as to her right to give a blessing. And another incident, a young priest, trying to guide a group of committed lay people, had them reciting the rosary together in the most dreary way and opposed any recitation of Prime or Compline since he felt, he said, that the Psalms were beyond their comprehension. We have come a long way since then, and priests and people have become at ease in the house of God together, offering the Holy Sacrifice of the Mass.

And as to the sacraments. When I visited Cuba and stayed with two American-educated Cubans who were wondering how they could have Christian Family meetings any longer without a priest, I called attention to the literature they could send for (the mails are still open between the United States and Cuba) and the two sacraments they could confer without a priest, the sacrament of Baptism and the sacrament of Matrimony. The marriage act itself is a sacrament, and grace is bestowed through it. And of course, as St. Teresa said, "All is grace."

To me the most significant thing Father McCarthy has said in this closely packed and reasoned and researched book, is this —and I quote the words at length because I do not think we can stress them enough:

. . . How much of the average priest's time is spent in celebrating Mass and administering the other sacraments? A quarter? A fifth? Probably not more than that. Moreover, with some obvious exceptions the administration of the sacraments is not overly difficult. A large part of it is mechanical and does not constitute a serious challenge. And it is precisely this—this lack of challenge in the priesthood understood as primarily a sac-

ramental ministry—that causes many young priests to question the value of their calling and to drift deeper and deeper into social work, psychology, or secular scholarship. But in doing this they may be making a mistake. For just as men have a right to good medicine from a doctor, and good legal counsel from a lawyer, so they have a right to a specific service from their priests and ministers. . . . I would say that . . . to contemplate and to communicate to others might serve as a grounding principle for the whole priestly ministry. To contemplate—both the Word of God and the word of man, both the city of God and the city of man—in order to unite the two, in order continually to renew the mystery of the Word made flesh. To contemplate not only books and ideas, but more especially people, the people we are called to live with and work for.

To read and to study . . . there should be much of this in the life of every priest so that he can penetrate more deeply into the mystery of the faith, to grow in the knowledge of God, our God who is a hidden God, and a consuming fire, our God who is the Word in Scripture, and the Word made flesh on the altar to feed us and strengthen us in this life of struggle.

For the priesthood of the laity there is no seminary to which we can go. So the preaching and teaching must take place in homes, on street corners, in store fronts, in every encounter. We have known many priests with this enthusiasm who shared the riches of their faith, shared their energy to work which these riches gave them. After all, if we lay folk do not *know* we have these riches, how are we going to use them? Our Father in heaven is a millionaire who has said to us in the Psalms, "Open your mouth and I will fill it."

If the priest from the richness of his own studies would convey to us some of the enthusiasm such studies engender, such light on the things of God, such strength to expect from participating in the Sacrifice, we might begin "to run in the way of His commandments," to love God and our brothers, and gather them with us on our way to God.

Charles Péguy has told us that when we come face to face with God He will say to us, "Where are the others?" We cannot find heaven here or hereafter alone. With Him all things are possible, and with "the others." All the way to heaven is heaven, St. Catherine of Siena told us, because He said "I am the Way."

DOROTHY DAY

Catholic Worker Farm
Epiphany 1967

THE POSTCONCILIAR CHRISTIAN

CONTENTS

INTRODUCTION

About four years ago, in an address of Cardinal Suhard's, I came across a short description of the "priesthood of the laity." No doubt I had seen the expression many times before, but this time it struck me as something new and important. And the more I read about it, the more convinced I became that this doctrine contained tremendous pastoral possibilities, and that a full understanding of it could provide laymen with a deeper vision of what it means to live in Christ. So I began to write down what I had been learning, and as I wrote, I was greatly encouraged by the fact that in Rome the same subject was being discussed and analyzed again and again by the Fathers of Vatican Council II.

Shortly thereafter the official decrees began to appear, and their statements both clarified and confirmed my own understanding of the layman's mission in the Church, and greatly enhanced its significance. The Constitution on the Sacred Liturgy of 1963 described the entire worship of the Church as "an exercise of the priestly office of Jesus Christ." The Constitution on the Church of 1964 contained a remarkably rich statement regarding the manner in which the layman actually carries out his priestly, prophetic, and royal mission. And finally, in 1965, the Decree on the Apostolate of the Laity went so far as to state that the layman possesses his apostolate in virtue of his share in Christ's royal and prophetic priesthood.

Inevitably the Council documents left much unsaid. Often they contained conclusions without developing or even mentioning the premises, and even the conclusions are so tersely stated that much remained to be done by way of explaining them and showing their full application. The purpose of this book is just that—to explore the premises and develop the conclusions of the Council decrees affecting the priesthood of the laity.

The book has five major sections: first, an introduction to the notions of priesthood and sacrifice; second, a description of the priesthood as it existed in Israel; third, a more thorough analysis of the priesthood of Christ himself; fourth, a study of the ways in which Christians participate in Christ's vocation; and finally, a consideration of the layman's apostolic ministry under three aspects—the prophetic, royal, and priestly.

This seemed to be the soundest approach to a sure understanding of the lay priesthood. For one thing, the priesthood of Christ cannot be fully appreciated unless seen against the backdrop of the priesthood in Israel; and moreover, the priesthood of Christians has neither meaning nor value apart from the priesthood of Christ. Christ is not only the source of the layman's priesthood; he is its exemplar as well.

Upon rereading the manuscript after having laid it aside for several months, I am satisfied that one can find here a theologically valid exposition of what it means to say that every Christian shares in Christ's royal and prophetical priesthood. And, if I may add without seeming to boast about my book, these pages are more than a report on what others have already said. In several places small but original advances in this area have been proposed—in, for example, my explanation of the sacerdotal dynamism in grace itself, and in my view of Baptism as the inaugural and directional sacrifice of the whole Christian life. Finally, this study has the advantage of being short. The layman has here a handbook in which he can acquire a theological appreciation of the way in which he has been called to continue Christ's work.

In conclusion I should like to express my gratitude to Father Valerian Thomas, O.P., who encouraged this work from beginning to end, and to Father Christopher Kiesling, O.P., for several insights on key points. For almost all quotations from Sacred Scripture the *Jerusalem Bible* version has been used, with the kind permission of the publishers, Doubleday and Company.

TIMOTHY MCCARTHY, O.P.

1 / PRIESTHOOD AND SACRIFICE

Protestants generally regard their clergy as "ministers," and primarily as ministers of the Word. Catholics, on the other hand, think of their clergy as "priests," and ordinarily regard the administration of the sacraments, particularly the offering of the Eucharist, as their principal function. Why this difference?

The answer lies in the way the two traditions understand the Eucharist. For the most part, Protestants view the Eucharist as a memorial of Christ's sacrifice, and not a sacrifice in itself. But for Catholics the Mass is a sacrifice, a sacramental sacrifice, a re-presentation, a re-enactment of the very same sacrifice that took place on Calvary. This being so, Catholics have no hesitation in calling their ministers "priests," for it is the function of a priest to offer sacrifice.

We mention this here only to bring out a point that will be of central importance throughout this study, namely, that priesthood and sacrifice are correlative realities. Where there is no sacrifice, there is no priesthood; and contrariwise, where there is no priesthood, there can be no sacrifice. By definition, a priest is a man qualified to offer sacrifice. Or, as the Epistle to the Hebrews puts it: "Every high priest has been taken out of mankind and is appointed to act for men in their relations with God, to offer gifts and sacrifices for sins" (Heb. 5:1).

Having said this, we wish to be equally emphatic in stating

that although the offering of sacrifice is the central and principal function of the priesthood, it is by no means its only function. Traditionally, a teaching or prophetic function and a ruling or pastoral function have also been involved in the priestly ministry. Nevertheless, these other functions are centered in and integrated around the climactic act of the priestly office, the offering of sacrifice.

The priest teaches and rules in order to prepare his community for sacrifice. Thus it was for Christ himself, and this is why he is most accurately described not as "priest, king, and prophet," as though these were three independent ministries, but rather as a "royal and prophetic high priest." Christ ruled, he taught, he offered sacrifice, but these were not three unrelated actions. He ruled and taught in order that men might profit from his sacrifice. His prophetic and royal actions converged (and still converge) upon his sacrifice.

In dividing Christ's ministry into these three functions we do not mean to imply that certain of Christ's acts were strictly prophetic, and others were only royal, and still others were purely sacrificial. No; for although in any given action of Christ's life one of these ministries usually predominated, all of his actions were at once prophetic, royal, and sacrificial. They were prophetic insofar as they were sign-giving and witness-bearing. They were royal or pastoral insofar as they were influential. They were sacrificial insofar as they were God-directed. Thus it was that Christ's death was at once a prophetic, pastoral, and sacrificial action *par excellence*. It was the culminating action of all three ministries.

Since the offering of sacrifice was central to the work of Christ, it is important that we understand exactly what sacrifice is; and here we must be careful to distinguish the various forms of sacrifice. Generically, a sacrifice is *a gift given to God*. It matters not what the gift is, nor why it is offered. So long as it is a true gift and so long as it is given to God, it is a sacrifice. Examples of what might be given are time, money, energy, freedom, life itself—anything that a man can call his own he can give to God. And he can make such gifts for a great variety of reasons—for example, because he loves, because he is sorry and wishes to atone, because he is grateful, because he worships, because he needs.

We said above that it is important to distinguish the various forms of sacrifice. Essentially there are only two: liturgical and nonliturgical. Formerly it was customary to characterize these two modes of sacrifice as external and internal, or material and spiritual. But this is misleading. For, first of all, every true external or visible sacrifice is also internal and spiritual. If it were not, it would be sheer formalism—an empty, soulless gesture. Secondly, a "spiritual" sacrifice may or may not be liturgical. The man who says a silent rosary is offering spiritual sacrifice, but not, however, a liturgical one. The same man when he goes to Mass is offering a sacrifice that is at once spiritual and material, internal and external.

A liturgical sacrifice is one that is given to God by an entire community through the ministration of an appointed member of that community, a priest. According to Catholic belief, this appointment can come only from God. "No one takes this honor on himself, but each one is called by God, as Aaron was" (Heb. 5:4). The gift offered by the community is a symbolic reality, symbolic of the community itself. In giving the gift, they are giving themselves. Once given, the offering "belongs" to God and can no longer be used for profane purposes.

A nonliturgical sacrifice, like a liturgical one, can be offered only by a priest appointed by God. We repeat, where there is no priest, there can be no sacrifice, liturgical or nonliturgical. If lay Christians were not priests, they could not offer any form of sacrifice. A nonliturgical sacrifice differs from its liturgical counterpart in that, strictly speaking, it is not offered by the whole community, but by an individual person for whatever particular reason he himself may choose.

Such sacrifices tend to be more informal and less symbolic. They tend to "hurt." A man gives away or gives up something to which he is attached, and in the giving, he experiences something of what Christ experienced on Calvary. For example, one may decide that during Lent he will rise thirty minutes earlier than usual in order to go to daily Mass. For the first few days this may be easy enough. But it won't be long before that dark March morning comes along when getting out of bed is like lifting a load of bricks.

In saying this I do not mean to say that pain itself constitutes a nonliturgical sacrifice. In reality the pain is only incidental. What matters is the gift itself, not the suffering. Nor is the value of the gift to be measured by how much difficulty we experience in giving it. Our Lord praised the woman who gave two mites not because it hurt her to give it, but because of the internal spirit that prompted it. In giving two mites, she was giving herself, and this is the essence of sacrifice. The suffering that is often connected with sacrifice is a result of our sinful condition, and not of sadistic desire on the part of God. Yet people sometimes seem to think that God is made happy when men make themselves unhappy for his sake, and that holiness and unhappiness are inextricably tied together.

Connected with this is the idea (still prevalent) that what constitutes a liturgical sacrifice is the *destruction* of the offering. As though God were pleased with destruction!

True enough, destruction often occurs within the ritual of liturgical sacrifice. Among the Jews, wine was poured out on the altar, incense was burned, animals were slain. But this was done not because God delighted in waste, but to symbolize the offerer's renunciation of something he possessed. To give is to surrender, to alienate, to break the relation a thing has to oneself. To symbolize this the offerer destroyed his offering. He spilled wine and killed animals to manifest the intensity of his desire that these gifts (symbolic of himself) belonged no longer to himself, but to God.

2 / PRIESTHOOD AND SACRIFICE
    IN ISRAEL

A. PRIESTHOOD IN ISRAEL

1. *Israel's National Priesthood*

In patriarchal times there was no special class of men set apart
for the performance of priestly functions. The patriarchs themselves offered sacrifice and conducted other religious rites.
Genesis states that after the flood subsided Noah built an altar
to the Lord and offered holocausts; and Abraham, upon receiving the Promise, offered sacrifice, as did Isaac and Jacob
when the Promise was later renewed to them.

The decisive moment in the history of Israel's priesthood
came when God spoke to Moses on Sinai. God said, "If you
obey my voice and hold fast to my covenant, you of all the
nations shall be my very own for all the earth is mine. I will
count you a *kingdom of priests,* a consecrated nation" (Exod.
19:5–6; emphasis added). When Moses came down from the
mountain, he asked the people whether they would accept
God's offer, and they responded, "All that Yahweh has said, we
will do." With that acceptance, they became, in the words of
Father Congar, "a consecrated people, a religious people, a
priestly and worshipping people." [1]

This was an unprecedented event in the history of religion.
Never before had an entire people been consecrated as priests.
And it was particularly significant that this *national priesthood*

13

antedated the institution of the *tribal priesthood* of the Levites. The Levites were chosen later, and they were chosen, not to substitute for the people, but to serve them. They were charged with the right and the responsibility of directing and fostering the worship of the whole nation. The Israelite ministerial priesthood (and subsequently the ministerial priesthood of Christianity) existed not for its own sake, but for the sake of the nation.

It is important to note that Israel became a priest by becoming a victim. In accepting the offer of Sinai, Israel handed over her corporate selfhood to God. Israel became his people, his possession. She was sacrificing herself; she was acting as both priest and victim. She offered; she was offered. Furthermore, she was binding herself to a sacrificial mode of existence, to a life of national self-oblation. One cannot separate Israel's priesthood from her victimhood. They are two sides of one coin.

When one views Israel's response to God at Sinai as a sacrificial action, the Law itself assumes a sacrificial character. In obeying the Law the Israelites were exercising their priesthood. They were actualizing their pledge to give themselves totally to God. Moreover, in adhering to the Law, the individual Israelite preserved that holiness and ritual purity without which he could not rightly participate in the nation's liturgy.

For Israel the Covenant on Sinai was a priestly *consecration*. Consecration implies reservation. After a chalice is consecrated it can no longer be used for nonreligious purposes, but only for the service of God. Similarly this people, being consecrated, belonged to God alone. Like a chalice, they were set aside for his service. Consecration also implies sacralization or divinization. As such, only God can consecrate. Only God can make holy. By reason of their priestly consecration the Israelites were sanctified, and consequently the sins they committed took on the added malice of sacrilege. In sinning they were profaning a reality that God had made sacred.

One can point to various differences between the priesthood of God's people in the Old Testament and that in the New. For one thing, priests under the Old Testament were *servants*, whereas those who share Christ's priesthood are *sons*, and their priestly service is a service of sons. For another, the national priesthood of the Old Testament was not "apostolic." Its entire movement was centripetal—toward the Temple, toward worship —rather than being, like that of the New, both centripetal and centrifugal, moving both toward God and toward men. Israel's sacerdotal ministry was only indirectly addressed to the world at large. Its aim was not so much to extend the Kingdom as it was to purify and strengthen it. In essence, her priestly service consisted in wholehearted complete obedience to the Law.

2. Israel's Tribal Priesthood

Acting on divine instruction, Moses consecrated Aaron and Aaron's sons as priests, and he prescribed that no one but they should perform this office. What were their duties? In the beginning their teaching function appears to have taken precedence over their strictly liturgical actions. Their primary responsibility was to teach the Law, and they were also custodians of the Urim and Thummim, the sacred lots by which the people sought God's will in particular matters. Not much is known about these lots, but it seems that in actual practice they did not differ very much from our custom of "flipping a coin." For example, on one occasion Saul used the lots to discover whether he and Jonathan or the whole people had sinned. He spoke: "If the fault lies on me or on my son Jonathan, O Yahweh, God of Israel, give Urim: if the fault lies on your people Israel, give Thummim" (I Sam. 14:41).

Their role in the liturgy arose from the fact that the ordinary Israelite was not permitted to enter the sanctuary, and therefore he needed sacerdotal assistance to bring his offerings and sacrifices to the altar. By David's time, the Urim and Thummim were no longer consulted and the task of teaching was gradually being pre-empted by Scribes and Teachers. This left the Levites with only one major function, and as the centuries passed they came to be more and more identified with liturgical activity alone. So much so, in fact, that when the Temple of Jerusalem was finally destroyed, Israel's priests found themselves with nothing left to do. It was as if doctors were suddenly placed in a world where people did not get ill. With the destruction of the Temple, writes Father De Vaux, "the religion of the Torah (Law) replaced the ritual of the Temple, and the priests were replaced by the rabbis." [2]

One might wonder why God should have established a tribal priesthood in addition to that of the whole nation. Why should men who are themselves priests be in need of further priests?

One answer to this question is contained in the adage that "where everyone is responsible, no one does the job." To take a modern example, if no one in a city is specifically assigned to keep the streets lighted, that community will be dark and dangerous at night. The same is true of religious duties. If no one were commissioned to provide for the maintenance and integrity of religious belief and practice, if worship were left to the autonomous inspiration of individual persons, the practice of religion would flounder even more seriously than it does now. Religion needs men whose whole lives are dedicated to it. Recognizing this need—indeed, having created it—God established a special, ministerial priesthood for his chosen people.

B. SACRIFICE IN ISRAEL

1. Israel's Sacrificial Rites

The Israelite liturgy included three distinct types of sacrifice: the holocaust (or burnt offering), the communion sacrifice (or peace offering), and expiatory sacrifices.

The word "holocaust" derives ultimately from the Hebrew word *olah*, which means "that which ascends." The holocaust was a sacrifice "which ascends" to the Lord—ascends in the form of smoke as it burns upon the altar. The distinctive feature of this sacrifice was that the entire victim was burnt, and no part of it was returned to the priest or offerer. The Old Testament is filled with examples of holocausts: Abraham offered one after the angel had stopped him from slaying his son; Gideon offered one when he had destroyed the altar of Baal; both David and Solomon offered them, David, when he established the Ark in Jerusalem, and Solomon, both before and after building the Temple.

Once the Temple liturgy was organized, holocausts were offered twice daily: in the morning and again at dusk. Larger holocausts were offered on Sabbath days, and still larger ones on the great feast days. On the first day of the Feast of Booths (the autumn feast celebrating the completion of the agricultural year) thirteen bullocks, two rams, and fourteen lambs were offered.

The rite began when the offerer solemnly placed his hands above the victim's head, thus indicating the "matter" of the sacrifice and indicating, too, that it was to be offered in his name. In private sacrifices the offerer himself killed the victim; in public or national sacrifices, this was done by the Levites. The blood, which the priests caught in a basin as it spurted from the animal's severed arteries, was poured out at the base of the altar. Then, the victim was skinned and quartered and placed upon the altar by the priest, there to burn until it was completely consumed.

Whereas the holocaust symbolized the total and unconditional character of man's response to God, the communion sacrifice symbolized Israel's relation to her Lord. The ritual for the communion sacrifice was very similar to that prescribed for holocausts, except that the victim was not wholly burnt. Only the kidneys, the liver, and the fatty parts around the intestines were placed in the flames. The breast and one of the legs went to the priests (the Hebrew stipend), and the rest went to the offerer, who then returned to his home, and there, in company with his family and friends, ate it at a sacred meal.

This meal was the climax of the communion sacrifice. It was a joyful affair, replete with hymns and several servings of wine. In eating the victim the people reminded themselves of their union with God and with one another, and pledged themselves to maintain and deepen this unity. It was a celebration of unity, an expression of intimate and harmonious fellowship between God and his people. Just as the Israelites sealed their human contracts by sharing a common meal, so here by eating the sacrificial victim they renewed their covenant agreement with Yahweh.

There were two kinds of expiatory sacrifices: offerings for sins and offerings of reparation. The exact difference between them is obscure, but we do know that monetary fines were usually attached to sacrifices of reparation, and it appears that such sacrifices were offered for social sins, sins that directly injured the rights of others. Sacrifices for sin covered a larger area, being offered for a great variety of faults, voluntary and involuntary.

It is noteworthy, however, that there were certain sins that no sacrifice could repair. Contempt of one's parents, adultery, incest, bestiality, Moloch worship (human sacrifice), and deliberate refusal to obey God's laws found no cure in sacrificial rites. Here, the voice of the prophets comforted the penitent sinner with promises the Law did not give. "Though your sins are like scarlet, they shall be as white as snow; though they are red as crimson, they shall be like wool. If you are willing to obey, you shall eat the good things of the earth" (Is. 1:18–19).

Two rites distinguished expiatory sacrifices: the solemnity attached to the blood ritual, and the final disposition of the victim. In the Hebrew mind, sin was associated with death. It was, as it were, a death-force. On the other hand, they linked blood with life. It was a life-force. In these sacrifices blood was smeared on the corners (the horns) of the altar and poured out at its base. In doing this, the sinner was symbolically reuniting his life (his blood) with God. The second distinguishing feature was the disposition of the victim. No part of the animal reverted to the offerer. One part was burned and the other and larger part went to the priests. This was because until the sacrifice was complete, the sinner remained in a state of legal impurity.

Such were the forms of sacrifice in Israel—forms that would find their fulfillment in the sacrifice of Christ. His sacrifice was a holocaust in that the Victim returned wholly to God. It was a communion sacrifice in that it brought into being a more intimate union between God and men than men would ever have hoped for. Finally, it was a sacrifice of expiation sufficient to atone for all the sins of the world.

2. The Prophets and Sacrifice

If the Law, and especially the Book of Leviticus, prescribed the external ritual for Israelite sacrifice, the prophets spoke of the spirit that should animate these offerings—and they did this in a most provocative way. They did it by condemning sacrifice. Listen to Amos, speaking for Yahweh:

I hate and despise your feasts,
I take no pleasure in your solemn festivals.
When you offer me holocausts, . . .
I reject your oblations,
*   and refuse to look at your sacrifices of fattened cattle.*
Let me have no more of the din of your chanting,
*   no more of your strumming on harps.*

[Amos 5:21 ff.]

Isaiah is no less severe:

What are your endless sacrifices to me?
*   says Yahweh.*
I am sick of holocausts of rams
*   and the fat of calves.*
The blood of bulls and of goats revolts me. . . .
Bring me your worthless offerings no more,
*   the smoke of them fills me with disgust.*
New Moons, sabbaths, assemblies—
I cannot endure festival and solemnity.

[Is. 1:11 ff.]

Jeremiah says: "Your holocausts are not acceptable, your sacrifices do not please me" (6:20). And Micah: "With what gift shall I come into Yahweh's presence and bow down before God on high? Shall I come with holocausts, with calves one year old? Will he be pleased with rams by the thousand, with libations of oil in torrents?" (6:6–7).

No, says the prophet. What God wants is not sacrifice, but justice, kindness, and humility. "What is good has been explained to you, man; this is what Yahweh asks of you: only this, to act justly, to love tenderly, and to walk humbly with your God" (6:8). Isaiah closes his diatribe against sacrifice with a plea for true religion: "Cease to do evil. Learn to do good, search for justice, help the oppressed, be just to the orphan, plead for the widow" (1:16–17). Hosea proclaims: "What I want is love, not sacrifice; knowledge of God, not holocausts" (6:6).

In these and other texts the prophets condemn not only sacrifice, but all the other externals of religion—public prayers, fasting, psalms, feasts. Some exegetes have claimed that these passages point to a definite break in Israel's religious consciousness. These texts, it is said, make it clear that Yahweh no longer desired external, ritual worship and that henceforth religion was to be something of the soul alone without involving public ceremonial. Recent studies of Hebrew thought idioms and literary genres, as well as the fact that in other passages these same prophets speak approvingly of the external aspect of Israel's worship, have rendered this position indefensible.

The prophets were preachers. When they saw their people sacrifice now to Yahweh and then to Baal, when they saw harlots attached to the sanctuaries, when they saw men offer sacrifice with one hand and shed blood with the other, when they saw the wealthy offer magnificent holocausts at the same time as they throttled the poor, they cried out against such worship with the whole force of their being. Sacrifice, as they saw it being practiced, was an evil and intolerable thing, an unholy and irreligious act, and they condemned it as such.

Most of all, they condemned it because the Israelites were worshiping Yahweh in the same way as the Canaanites worshiped Baal. They were using ritual as a *substitute* for morality. They were acting as though ceremonial were all that God demanded. They were offering sacrifice as though God's rewards and punishments depended upon the largess of a man's external offerings. In short, sacrifice was becoming superstition.

To bring an end to this, the prophets resorted to a Semitic form of hyperbole. In effect they said "never that, only this," in order to say "this is more important than that." They painted in black and white without giving exact shades. Our Lord himself used this method many times. He said: "He who receives me, receives *not me,* but him who sent me." He said: *"Work not* for the food that perishes, but for the food that affords eternal life." He said: "If any man comes to me without *hating* his father and mother . . . , he can be no disciple of mine."

In these passages Christ was not condemning love of parents or secular work. He was saying only that there are things more important than these. Similarly, the prophets said "righteousness only" in order to make it emphatically clear that "righteousness is more important than ritual." They were saying exactly what Samuel said in the First Book of Samuel: "Obedience is better than sacrifice, submissiveness better than the fat of rams" (15:22).

Nor is this the only lesson that the prophets taught about sacrifice. For to them sacrifice was not confined to what men did in the Temple at Jerusalem. It included such things as acts of mercy, avoidance of sin, a contrite heart, an act of thanksgiving wherever and whenever made, and living one's life in humble submission to God. Sirach put it this way:

A man multiplies offerings by keeping the Law;
*   he offers communion sacrifices by following the commandments.*
By showing gratitude he makes an offering of fine flour,
*   by giving alms he offers a sacrifice of praise.*
Withdraw from wickedness and the Lord will be pleased,
*   withdraw from injustice and you make atonement.*

[Sir. 35:1–5]

Through these and similar texts the Prophetical and Wisdom literature of the Old Testament provided St. Augustine with the scriptural foundation for his classic definition of sacrifice: "True sacrifice is every work done with the aim of uniting us with God in a holy fellowship, that is to say, every work that has as its end that Good which alone can make us truly blessed." [3]

3 / JESUS CHRIST:
ROYAL AND PROPHETIC HIGH PRIEST

With this chapter we take a long step forward in our search for sources for the priesthood of the laity. We shall explore the priesthood of Christ under four heads: his priestly vocation, his "ordination," his sacrifice, his priestly ministry in heaven.

A. THE PRIESTLY VOCATION OF CHRIST

1. *In the Old Testament*

What does the Old Testament say about Christ? There are two ways to answer this question. The first is to try to get inside the minds of the Israelites themselves, and to examine the scriptural content of their messianic hopes. If we were to do this, we would find that these hopes, though certain, were somewhat vague and confused, perhaps analogous to our own expectations of the Second Coming. We know that Christ will come again, but when and where and how and in exactly what manner we do not know. Nor are we sure exactly how literally to take certain of Christ's affirmations in regard to this *Parousia*.

A second way to approach the Old Testament is to view it in the light of what actually happened in the New. This is a traditional and valid procedure. As St. Augustine said, God wisely arranged not only that the New Testament be hidden in the Old, but that the Old be made manifest in the New. And the Vatican II Constitution on Divine Revelation makes the same point when it states that the Old Testament acquires and sheds forth its full meaning only in the New Testament. Seen then in this way, what does the Old Testament say of Christ?

We see that no sooner had Adam fallen than he was promised a *conqueror* who would undo the evil into which sin had cast him. This original promise was gradually expanded upon down through the centuries. To Abraham, God promised an heir through whom all the nations would be blessed. To Moses he promised that in the sometime future he would raise up "a prophet like yourself. . . . I shall put my words into his mouth and he shall tell them all I command him" (Deut. 18:18). To David, he promised a *successor-king* whose dynasty would remain forever unshaken. And Psalm 110 adds that this savior would be "a *priest* of the order of Melchizedek, and for ever."

King, prophet, and priest though he was destined to be, he would also be the "scorn of mankind," the "jest" of his people (Ps. 22:6). Enemies would ring him round; his life would be spent as spilt water; his bones would be ripped from their joints; holes would be torn in his hands and feet. Yet, somehow, he would be delivered from his misery, and live on in his (God's) presence, and beget children to serve him (Ps. 22:30). For his part, the Messiah would have only one desire—to do the will of Yahweh. "Here I am! I am coming! In the scroll of the book am I not commanded to obey your will? My God, I have always loved your Law from the depths of my being" (Ps. 40:7–8).

During the four centuries from the schism of Israel and Judah (931) to the Babylonian Captivity (587), God raised up a long line of prophets who made significant contributions to the overall picture of what the future Messiah would do. Hosea, in the eighth century, foretold that Judah and Israel would be rallied under a *ruler* of their common choice, and come flocking back to Jerusalem from every corner of the land. On that day, the

Lord would bring healing to their crushed spirits and in free mercy give them back his love.

Isaiah, also eighth century, spoke of one who would be a *light* to men walking in darkness and a *signal* beckoning to people all around. The Gentiles would pay him homage. He would be a *king* who loved righteousness, a *judge* who would give speedy redress, a *savior* who would deliver his people from Egypt (symbol of slavery and bondage).

Micah, also eighth century, spoke of a *shepherd* who would safely guard his flock and a *prince* whose fame would reach to the ends of the world. And Psalm 71, thought to be written at about this time, says that the Messiah would found a kingdom of peace, and it stresses the universality of his domain. "His empire shall stretch from sea to sea, . . . all kings will do him homage, all nations become his servants" (Ps. 72:8, 11).

Jeremiah, sixth century, told of a *king* who would rule all Israel, and whose posterity would be "as the array of heaven [which] is past counting" (33:22). Through him, a new covenant would be made with Yahweh, a covenant that would last forever, that would be engraved not on stones, but written upon the hearts of men. By means of this covenant, the guilt of Israel would be purged away and all their wrongs would be forgiven. Jeremiah stressed the redemptive character of the Messiah's mission.

Ezekiel, sixth century, spoke about a *shepherd* who would reunite his flock, and a *king* who would rule forever. He too foresaw a new covenant, new hearts, a new law, a new spirit. Through Second-Isaiah, that anonymous sixth-century Israelite who added his own inspired message to the writings of one whose spirit he shared, we learn of a mysterious "servant" who would proclaim right order among the Gentiles, give sight to the blind, set the prisoner free, and proclaim the day of the Lord's pardon. Through him salvation would go out to the farthest corners of the earth. And yet, no one would be so despised, so mishandled, so crushed, so wounded. But through his sufferings a multitude of nations would be purified; his bruises would be our healing; his suffering would take away our guilt. His acceptance of torment and torture would enable him to claim many as his own.

The later prophets, with the exception of Daniel, added little to the developing picture of the Messiah. Daniel told of a vision in which he saw a "son of man" riding on the clouds of heaven, one to whom was given universal power and glory. "On him was conferred sovereignty, glory and kingship, and men of all peoples, nations and languages became his servants" (7:14).

This vision was the final stroke, as it were, in the Old Testament painting of the Messiah. What, in retrospect, did it tell us? It told us, first of all, that he would be a *savior*—a savior of his race, a savior of all nations. It told us that he would be a *prophet*, a teacher, a light to Jews and Gentiles alike, and it told us that he would be a *king*, like David, but greater than David, for his empire would last forever and his power would stretch to the uttermost bounds of the earth.

Finally, it told us that he would be a *priest* whose priesthood would last forever. Yet, for all these titles, he would be Yahweh's suffering servant, a man despised, abject, unwanted, a man who would undergo horrible pain and death itself, but whose sufferings would be a source of blessings for all.

Such is the Old Testament picture of Christ. All the elements are there, but they are not yet integrated, not yet balanced. It was not yet known how one man would unite in himself all these roles. To know this we must turn from the promise to the reality—to the works and words of Christ himself.

2. In the Gospels

What did Christ himself consider his mission to be? Basically he regarded it as a work of fidelity and obedience. He often returned to this theme, particularly in St. John's account. Thus,

"I have come from heaven, not to do my own will, but to do the will of the one who sent me" (6:38). "Am I not to drink the cup that the Father has given me?" (18:11). "My food is to do the will of the one who sent me, and to complete his work" (4:34). "I always do what pleases him" (8:29). "I must carry out the work of the one who sent me" (9:4). "What the Father has taught me is what I preach" (8:29). "For what I have spoken does not come from myself; no, what I was to say, what I had to speak, was commanded by the Father who sent me" (12:49).

We know, then, that Christ conceived of his mission in terms of obedience. But what was the nature and the direction of the obedience to which he bound himself? The answer to this question is contained both in Christ's deeds and in his words.

Looking at Christ's life as a totality, we see, first of all, that he was a teacher of surpassing skill. By far the largest portion of his public ministry was devoted to teaching and evangelizing. He even thought of himself as a prophet. Referring to himself, he said: "I tell you solemnly, no prophet is ever accepted in his own country" (Luke 4:24). Furthermore, his contemporaries commonly regarded him as a man of the word, as a prophet, rather than as a king or priest. "And when he entered Jerusalem, the whole city was in turmoil. 'Who is this?' people asked. And the crowds answered, 'This is the prophet Jesus from Nazareth in Galilee' " (Matt. 20:10–11).

Secondly, Christ was a man of power, unique power, power over death and disease, power over men's hearts, power over evil spirits, power over the things of nature—bread, water, wind, wine. And he was a leader of exceptional genius, the surest proof of which is the fact that the very same community that he founded two thousand years ago continues to exist today. A prophet, a man of great power, a charismatic leader— such was Christ's image among those with whom he lived.

Now to Christ's own words. How did he describe his mission? One of the most significant texts on this point is given by St.

Matthew: "Do not imagine that I have come to abolish the Law or the prophets; I have come not to abolish but to complete them" (5:17). Here, Christ was declaring himself to be the fulfillment of the Old Testament messianic prophecies. Here, implicitly, he was claiming to be the savior promised to Adam, the prophet promised to Moses, the priest of whom the Psalmist spoke, and the king of whom so much was said.

But Christ told us not only that he was the fulfillment to whom the prophets pointed; he told us also of the manner in which he would integrate the many works and offices that the prophets mentioned. He did this, first of all, by giving us a sharp, clear picture of the general purpose and focus of his work. "The son of man," he said, "did not come to be served but to serve, *and to give his life as a ransom for many*" (Mark 10:45; emphasis added). Here, Christ centered in on the ultimate reason for his human existence. He came to free men, to ransom them from their captivity to sin and death and Satan, and he would do this through his death, by giving his life.

Christ always spoke of his death as the critical moment of his existence. He called it his "cup," his "time," his "hour." He likened it to a baptism of suffering into which he must plunge. "There is a baptism I must still receive, and how great is my distress till it is over!" (Luke 12:50). Through this baptism men would be redeemed, through it he would draw all things to himself, through it he would, like a grain of wheat fallen into the ground, bear much fruit.

Do these and other texts suggest that Christ regarded his death as the end of his ministry? On the cross Christ said, "It is finished"; and truly something was finished. His work of atonement and merit was finished. Having died once, he would die no more. But there still remained the work of applying this merit and forgiveness to men down through the ages, a work that would last till the end of time. Thus it was that Christ promised his disciples that once he was in heaven, he would send them his Spirit, and would be with them, active and effective, all days even to the end of the world.

When that end was finally to come, he would return in glory, power, and majesty; he would gather all the nations of the world before him, and separate the sheep from the goats, saying to those on his right, "Come, you whom my Father has blessed, take for your heritage the kingdom prepared for you since the foundation of the world." And to those on his left: "Go away from me, with your curse upon you, to the eternal fire prepared for the devil and his angels" (Matt. 25:34 f., 41 f.). Only then, when the final judgment is rendered, will Christ's mission have come to an end. Only then will salvation history have reached its term.

In summary, Christ's works and words give us, first of all, a more exact, more refined intuition into the ultimate purpose of his coming—man's redemption. Secondly, they make it clear that Christ's death and resurrection were crucial to the fulfillment of this work. Thirdly, they tell us that Christ's work was not to end with his death, but was to continue till the Second Coming and the Final Judgment.

Thus we begin to see how the various elements of Christ's vocation fit together. To see this still more clearly, let us turn to the writings of three men whose adult lives were spent contemplating the mystery of Christ—to Paul, Peter, and John.

3. *In the Epistles of St. Paul, St. Peter, and St. John*

For Paul, Christ was a man "put forward" by God, "sent" by God, "appointed" by the Father. He was both God's ambassador to men and man's representative with God. He was, in short, a mediator, *the* mediator. "There is only one God, and there is only one mediator between God and mankind, himself a man, Christ Jesus" (I Tim. 2:5). As a mediator, his work was one of reconciliation. "God in Christ," wrote Paul to the Corinthians, "was reconciling the world to himself" (II Cor. 5:19).

To effect this work, Christ had to pay the price stipulated by his Father; he had to humble himself, assume the status of a slave, and become obedient, even unto death. More than anything else, it was Christ's filial obedience that reconciled men to God. "As by one man's disobedience many were made sinners, so by one man's obedience many will be made righteous" (Rom. 5:19).

Although everything that Christ did was done for our redemption and although each of his acts was truly redemptive, God willed that one particular act of obedience should be the means whereby men would be restored to God's love. This was Christ's pasch, his death. In Paul's terms, it was the "cross" that saved us, the "cross" that erased the handwriting that was against us.

God signaled his acceptance of Christ's redemptive action on Calvary by raising him from the dead. Once risen, he became a "life-giving Spirit," a living source of redemption to all who would call upon him. He took his place at the Father's right hand, where he continues his saving work, always interceding for us. There he lives on as our advocate with God, his humanity having become the living instrument through which all grace comes to men.

Therefore it is the living, risen, glorified Christ in whom men must place their hope. "If Christ has not been raised then our preaching is useless, and your believing it is useless" (I Cor. 15:14). It is the living, risen Christ that saves; the living, risen Christ who transforms into his own image those who believe. Paul, more than any other apostolic writer, emphasized the fact that Christ's saving mission, far from ending on Good Friday or Easter Sunday, in a sense only began then. Then, he was the Lord, the Kyrios, into whose hands God had given all power on heaven and earth.

In the Epistle to the Hebrews, most probably not written by

Paul but by someone profoundly influenced by him, the whole mystery of Christ is subsumed under his priesthood. Christ is portrayed as the divinely commissioned high priest of the human race come to offer a sacrifice that would secure eternal redemption for all men. In virtue of this sacrifice, Christ has passed through the heavens and entered into the Holy Place, the true Holy of Holies, not made by hands, and there he will continue to exercise his priestly ministry until the Parousia.

The Johannine writings and those attributed to Peter add the final touches to our picture. Peter speaks of Christ as being a sacrificial victim, likening him to a "lamb without spot or stain" (I Peter 1:19). John lays special emphasis on the fact that Christ's redemptive mission was a work of love. "God loved the world so much that he gave his only son . . ." (John 3:16). And again, "This is the love I mean: not our love for God, but God's love for us when he sent his Son to be the sacrifice that takes our sins away" (I John 4:10). The Book of Revelation also refers to Christ as a "Lamb"—"the Lamb who was slain." And in one of the visions recounted there, Christ is seen clothed in priestly robes. Thus in the same book Christ is presented as both the eternal priest and the eternal victim.

B. THE PRIESTLY CONSECRATION OF CHRIST

1. *The Incarnation*

Jesus Christ is mankind's high priest. The Epistle to the Hebrews calls him "the apostle and high priest of our religion," "a priest of the order of Melchizedek and for ever," "a compassionate and trustworthy high priest of God's religion," "the high priest of all the blessings which were to come" (3:1; 5:6; 2:17; 8:11). Christ is not simply a priest among other priests, greater than they or more holy. He is *the* priest. Other men are priests only to the extent that they share in his priesthood. For Christians there is only one priesthood and one sacrifice—the priesthood and sacrifice of Jesus Christ.

Christ's priestly "ordination" was the Incarnation. He became a priest at the same moment that he *as man* became God's son. In fact, his sonship *is* his priesthood. Because he is God's son, and uniquely so, he can take his place at the head of the human race to intercede for all with his Father. His sonship is the source of his acceptability with God and of his ability to offer an acceptable sacrifice. Later we shall see that we, like Christ, are made priests by being made sons, adopted sons of God. *The root of all priesthood is a filial relation between God and man.*

In the Old Testament only the high priest was anointed with oil. The other assisting priests were sprinkled with lustral water. Christ's humanity was anointed with divinity itself. St. John Damascene writes: "The unction of his humanity is his divinity." [4] This unction permeated him totally, and it did so in two distinct ways: through the Hypostatic Union and through the charity or grace that filled his soul.

By reason of the Hypostatic Union (the substantial union of his human nature with the divine nature of the Word), the man Christ was raised infinitely above every other man so that he alone could act as man's rightful representative before God. By reason of his grace (the divine love that permeated his soul), he was, as it were, "compelled" to activate his priesthood and to effect the work of reconciliation to which he was called.

Thus it can be said that the Hypostatic Union constituted or established Christ as priest, and that grace, his divine love for both God and men, was the fuel that fired his priestly ministry. Father Héris states it this way: "Christ, in virtue of the Hypostatic Union, *is* priest, but he still lacks the faculties which enable him to *act* as priest. He receives these faculties by the infusion of sanctifying grace." [5] An analogous combination is effected by the sacrament of Baptism. The baptismal character consecrates the Christian as a priest, and the grace of the sacrament incites and empowers him to fulfill his priestly ministry.

Although Christ's divinity is the underlying reason for the efficaciousness of his priesthood, his priestly actions were human actions, not divine ones. A priest is one who prays, adores, worships, offers sacrifice. Christ, as God, could not do these things. Only one who is an inferior can pray and worship and adore. Therefore, Christ's humanity is no mere accessory to his priesthood; it is its very foundation. How perfectly the Incarnation fitted Christ for his mission: because he was human, he could humble himself before God; because he was human, he could offer sacrifice; and because he was God, his prayer could not help but be acceptable to the Father.

Christ's solidarity with the human race enabled him to know our condition firsthand. Before his incarnation, the Word of God knew the "ups and downs" of human life from the serenity of divine contemplation. After the Incarnation, he knew of them from his own experience.

There is only one aspect of life of which Christ had no experience, and that is sin. He was tempted, but he never sinned. But this, far from separating him from us, rendered him all the closer. For it is sin that isolates and hardens men and makes them insensitive and indifferent to one another. The holier a man is, the more he is freed from egoism, and the greater is his capacity for love and empathy. Christ's holiness was absolute. The barriers that keep men apart—fear, pride, envy, self-seeking—had no hold on him.

The Epistle to the Hebrews points up the excellence of Christ's priesthood by comparing it to the Levitical priesthood. Unlike the Levites, Christ possessed his priesthood by a personal title rather than a hereditary one, and he possessed it forever, whereas the Levites possessed theirs only during their lives. "Then there used to be a great number of those other priests, because death put an end to each one of them; but this one, because he remains *for ever*, can never lose his priesthood" (Heb. 7:23–24). Moreover, Jesus, being sinless, had no need to "offer sacrifice every day, as the other high priests do for their own sins and then for those of the people, because he has done this once and for all by offering himself" (7:27).

The priests of the Old Law approached God as sinners; the one high priest of the New Law was "holy, innocent and uncontaminated, beyond the influence of sinners" (7:26). The very abolition of the old priesthood was an indication of its inherent imperfection. If it had been perfect, there would have been no need for a change. "If that first covenant had been without a fault, there would have been no need for a second one to replace it" (8:7). Similarly, "If perfection had been reached through the levitical priesthood . . . , why was it still necessary for a new priesthood to arise . . . ?" (7:11).

Finally, the priesthood of Christ offers men a fuller hope, a hope of eternal salvation to those who will make their way to God through him.

2. *The Baptism in the Jordan*

The Incarnation was not Christ's only priestly consecration. He received a second priestly anointing when the Holy Spirit descended upon him immediately after his baptism.

Exegetes have not always agreed regarding the significance of Christ's baptism. Some, like Loisy and Wellhausen, held that it was the transforming experience of his whole life; the moment when he perceived himself to be uniquely related to God; the event that convinced him of his messiah-ship. Others regard the whole incident as purely symbolic, a sign that Christ's hidden life was over and that his public ministry was about to begin, a sign that had no real effect upon Christ.

The baptism administered by John was a baptism of penance,

and for this reason it is difficult to see why Christ should have received it. John himself sensed the incongruity: "It is I who need baptism from you . . . and yet you come to me!" (Matt. 3:14). To this Jesus answered: "Leave it like this for the time being; it is fitting that we should, in this way, do all that righteousness demands" (3:15). The "righteousness" of which Christ spoke here was the preordination of the event by the Father. In being baptized, Jesus was walking the path his Father had marked out for him. But why should this road have included such an event? What was its meaning?

Some see in it a fulfillment of prophecy. Isaiah had said in his fourth Servant Song that the future Messiah would "be counted among the wrong-doers." By being baptized, Christ was identifying himself with sinners—with those to whom John said, "I baptize you in water, for repentance" (Matt. 3:11).

Another explanation links his baptism with the Circumcision and the Presentation in the Temple. All three of these events marked Christ as a member of his people. By being circumcised and presented in the Temple, he entered the religious community of Israel. By being baptized, he entered the group that represented the purest strain of the old order. John the Baptist was the authentic prophet for the closing days of the old dispensation. The Jews who accepted his baptism were drawn up to the ultimate disposition for receiving the long-awaited Messiah.

Immediately after his baptism Jesus came up out of the water and began to pray; and while he was praying the heavens opened, "and the Holy Spirit descended upon him in bodily form as a dove" (Luke 3:22). In the Acts of the Apostles this descent of the Spirit is called an anointing. "You must have heard about the recent happenings in Judaea; about Jesus of Nazareth and how he began in Galilee, after John had been preaching baptism. *God had anointed him with the Holy Spirit* and with power, and because God was with him, Jesus went about doing good and curing all who had fallen into the power of the devil" (Acts 10:37–38).

St. Jerome, commenting on this passage, says: "This was a spiritual unction, not a material one as was given to the *Jewish priests,*" thus implying that he regarded this as a sacerdotal anointing.[6] St. Peter Damien is more explicit: "When this dove descended upon the Lord after the Baptism, Jesus . . . received the rights of the true priesthood." [7] On the other hand, some scholars hold that, strictly speaking, this was not a sacerdotal anointing, but a prophetic one. "The unction which he received," writes Father De la Potterie, "is presented as a prophetic one. Nothing indicates that it was royal or sacerdotal." [8]

While I agree that this anointing did prepare Christ for his prophetic work, I do not see that this was its only purpose. The Holy Spirit was here preparing Christ for the whole of his ministry—a ministry that was not merely prophetic, or merely kingly, or merely priestly, but was rather an integration of all three, and an integration centered in his priesthood. This anointing, like that of the Incarnation, was fundamentally sacerdotal.

The question remains as to whether the Spirit's descent was merely symbolic or whether it truly had an effect upon Christ. No doubt it was symbolic. It was a sign given to John (and perhaps to others as well) that Jesus was the elect of God, and that the Spirit of God would be with him in his work. But was it more than this? The evidence seems to indicate that it was, and that we have here a real communication of the Holy Spirit, an illumination, an apostolic impulsion that Christ received to commence his public life, a spiritual impetus for his future work.

Père Lagrange believes that at the Jordan Christ did not receive an increase in sanctifying grace, but a special supernatural charism for the performance of his ministry, something similar to what we would call the "grace of office." Luke wrote that after the anointing, the Spirit *drove* Christ into the desert, and Mark says that after it, "Jesus came back into Galilee *with the power of the Spirit upon him*." "One gets the impression," writes Father Lecuyer, "that after the baptism Jesus is more immediately moved and guided by the Spirit than he was before." [9]

What powers were contained in this charism? Jesus himself tells us when, upon returning to his synagogue at Nazareth, he applied a passage from Isaiah to himself:

The spirit of the Lord has been given to me,
   for he has anointed me.
He has sent me to bring the good news to the poor,
   to proclaim liberty to captives
   and to the blind new sight,
   to set the downtrodden free,
   to proclaim the Lord's year of favour.

[Luke 4:18–19]

When Isaiah first spoke these words, he was speaking to a captive people, and he was telling them that a savior was coming who would release them from their captivity. Jesus was here claiming to be that savior. And yet, the saving work to which he was called was far more profound than that of liberating captives of war. It was an ultimate liberation, a liberation from sin and death, a liberation from everything that enslaved man and made it impossible for him to live in union with God.

The Fathers of the Church likened Christ's liberating work to that of Moses. Like Moses, he brought a people from slavery to freedom; like him, he went out into the desert and was there tempted; like him also, he announced to his people the good news of their entrance into the Promised Land. But there were differences, too. Jesus came to liberate all men and not just the

Jews, and he was leading men from a far more oppressive slavery and to a far more exalted freedom than was Moses. Furthermore, while Moses had died without entering the Promised Land, Jesus entered it at the head of his brethren. Finally, Jesus freed men from the very Law that Moses had given them. "Though the Law was given through Moses, grace and truth have come through Jesus Christ" (John 1:17).

This all-embracing work of liberation would be accomplished through the action of the Holy Spirit. This work would involve preaching and teaching, ruling and guiding, healing and exorcising, organizing and planning; but all these activities would be centered in his sacrifice. Christ's first baptism was connected with his second, with his baptism on the cross. The first initiated, the second consummated his priestly ministry.

C. THE SACRIFICE OF CHRIST

As we have already seen, a sacrifice is a gift given to God. In the broad sense, it can be any action done for God, directly or indirectly, implicitly or explicitly. In the strict sense, it is a liturgical action in which some material object is handed over to God as an expression of a people's self-offering. The acceptability of a sacrifice depends not on the external offering but upon the acceptability of the offerer himself. Abel's sacrifice was preferred to that of Cain not because God preferred animal offerings to vegetable ones but because Abel was a just man and Cain was not.

During his life on earth Jesus offered sacrifice in both the wide sense and the strict sense. In the next few pages we shall analyze these offerings both interiorly and exteriorly. We shall consider, first of all, Christ's spiritual sacrifice; then, his sacrifice on Calvary; and finally, the sacrifice he offered at the Last Supper.

1. *Christ's Spiritual Sacrifice*

To offer spiritual sacrifice a man must have at least a minimal awareness that he is related to God. The more perfectly he understands and appreciates this relation, the more deeply will he desire to offer such sacrifice. Since no one was more profoundly aware of his relation with God than Jesus Christ, he was of all human beings most disposed to offer sacrifice.

It may be said of Christ, as of no one else, that he realized to the full what it means to be a creature. He had a living awareness that his moment-to-moment existence depended upon the sustaining power of God. He knew that if God were to will it, he would vanish in an instant. He knew that everything in him—his every wish, dream, thought, hope and desire—had been foreknown and forewilled by God. And more than this, he knew that of all God's creatures he had been blessed the most. God loved him more than any other man. He had been given more knowledge. He had been completely removed from sin and all its debilitating effects. His humanity had been assumed by the divine personality of the Word. Realizing these things, he was moved to surrender himself completely back to God. He made this surrender at the first moment of his existence. "And this is what he said, on coming into the world":

You who wanted no sacrifice or oblation
*   prepared a body for me.*
You took no pleasure in holocausts or sacrifices for sin;
*   then I said,*
*   just as I was commanded in the scroll of the book,*
'God, here I am! I am coming to obey your will.'

[Heb. 10:5–7]

This was the beginning of Christ's spiritual sacrifice.

Christ gave himself completely and utterly. There was

nothing that he kept for himself, nothing that he held back. For us who bear the marks of original and personal sin, such a total gift is impossible. We do not have sufficient power over ourselves to make it. However generous we may be at one moment, there is always some trace of egoism, some streak of possessiveness, some weakness of the flesh or spirit, that withdraws the gift. Only Christ and his blessed Mother, being sinless, had the power to offer themselves in total holocaust to God.

Christ's gift of himself was not simply the gift of a creature to his Creator. More especially, it was the gift of a son to his Father. Christ's whole approach to God was filial, and all of his Godward actions bore the impress of filial love and filial reverence. This love was unreserved and unconditional, a complete outpouring of self, a complete emptying of self. All his powers, energies, and talents were oriented toward his Father, toward his Father's glory, toward his will, toward his holy name.

If Christ's love for his Father was filial, so also was his obedience. The obedience of a son differs from that of a subject. A son comes to "sense" his father's will; he comes to know it instinctively. There is nothing insecure or anxious about such obedience. It is confident, free, and expansive. A son knows that no matter what he might do, his father will not cease loving him. So it was with Christ. The Gospels show that Christ's one great desire in life was to do his Father's will. This was his "food and drink." If Christ can be said to have had a "philosophy of life," that philosophy centered upon loving obedience to his Father.

Christ's approach to God was filial; his approach to men was fraternal. He was as human (truly, he was more human) as we are, and he thought of himself as such. This made him accessible and available to men. This meant that he loved being with them, that he enjoyed their company, appreciated their humor, and desired their love. It meant that he was sensitive to individual differences, and that he never responded to any two people in exactly the same way. Each was a brother, and for each he would not hesitate to die; yet each was an individual with his own strengths and weaknesses, his own joys and sorrows, his own past, present, and future. Christ calls each by his first name.

He not only loved his fellow men; he also recognized his responsibility toward them. He knew that his Father had placed him at the head of humanity, and he knew that he was responsible for the salvation of his human brothers. Conscious of these things and motivated by love, he went forth on his mission of mercy with set purpose and with joy. Nothing could deter him from accomplishing the work with which he had been entrusted. The devil tried three times and failed.

Aware of where he stood both in relation to God and in relation to men, Christ offered every act to God as a spiritual sacrifice for the salvation of men. Whatever he did, whatever he experienced, whatever he said or thought—all was given to God. Whether it was the labors he shared with Joseph in Nazareth, or the journeys he made to the Temple, or the care he took for his mother; whether it was his incessant travels, or his physical exhaustion, or the taunts and misunderstandings that followed him everywhere—all these things were part of his total holocaust.

And because they were the actions of a man who had been established as humanity's advocate with God, all of them contributed to man's salvation. Each of them in its own way merited grace for mankind. Indeed, since each of these actions was performed by a man who was also God, any one of them would have been more than sufficient to satisfy for the sins of the whole human race. But God willed that salvation should come to men through one particular sacrifice that was symbolic as well as spiritual. He willed that men should be saved through the sacrifice of the cross.

2. The Sacrifice of the Cross

Since every action of Christ was perfect interiorly and exteriorly, why should God have singled out his passion and death as the means whereby men would be reunited to him?

St. Augustine offered a psychological answer. He said that men find it far more difficult to offer love than to respond to it, and that in the cross of Christ we have the ultimate revelation, the ultimate sign of the depth of God's love for us. The man who cannot love a brother who died for him is a callous, insensitive soul. Anyone who meditates upon the mystery of the cross and sees it for what it truly is, is almost compelled to return the love which it expresses. And since men are saved by loving God in Christ, Calvary was perfectly adapted toward achieving its divinely instituted purpose.

This was, however, not the only reason for the cross. By dying an undeserved death, Christ broke through the power of death. By passing from death to life, he gave death its true meaning. He showed that it was not only an end, but a transition, an opening out of one life into another. As we read in the Preface of the Mass for the Dead, "Unto the faithful, life is changed, not taken away."

Another reason God established his final covenant with men upon Calvary was that he desired to center Christian worship in this action. A sacrificial act, symbolic of harmonious interaction between God and man, was supremely suited to fulfill this purpose. Through such an action men, in Christ, could give themselves to God, and God, also in Christ, could give himself to men. Christ's ascending and descending mediation could be united in one work. And thus this work could unify and focus the whole of Christian life. It could become the axis toward which everything else would converge.

Whatever reasons we can see for the supreme efficaciousness of the cross, it remains a fact of faith that God willed it this way. The New Testament clearly affirms that the cross put an end to the Law, reconciled men with God, broke down the wall that separated Jew and Gentile, established peace between God and the human race, took away the curse that was against us, and enabled men to receive God's love and thereby become his children and heirs.

The cross was, therefore, the key reality in Christ's life. It was his "hour," the decisive act of his earthly existence. From the beginning of his public life (if not before), its specter impressed itself upon his consciousness. He foresaw every aspect of his passion—the scourging, the mockery, the crucifixion. He foresaw these things, accepted them, went forward to them. Three times he predicted his passion.

Imagine the fear and trepidation that would build up in our hearts if we knew the day, the moment, the causes, and every circumstance of our death, and imagine how this agony would multiply as we approached the end. About such matters a measure of ignorance is a blessing from God. But because Christ's death was destined to be a sacrifice, he had to be completely conscious of what he was doing and what he was giving. Otherwise his sacrifice would have been less than human.

All of Christ's actions merited grace for men, but only the cross brought salvation. The redemptive value of his earlier actions was conditioned by and dependent upon his final action. The offering that he made upon Calvary was, as it were, the deathblow that he administered to Satan and sin. Until that blow was delivered, Satan held men in his grasp. Christ's earlier actions—his miracles, his prayers, his teaching—were like the opening skirmishes of a war. Christ won them all, and all of them were conducive to his ultimate victory; but that victory was not won until he gave up his spirit upon the cross.

Christ's action upon Calvary contained all of the elements of a liturgical sacrifice. In it a visible gift was given to God as an outward expression of interior self-surrender. The gift that he gave was his physical human life. And this was the sign of the invisible gift of his whole human self. In Old Testament sacrifices the external gift and the internal gift were two separate realities. The offerer offered a goat, or a ram, or a sheep. But in Christ's sacrifice the internal and external offerings were one reality—Christ himself.

The entire act was voluntary. No one took Christ's life away from him. He laid it down of his own accord. "No one takes it from me, I lay it down of my own free will" (John 11:18). An ordinary man cannot do this in the way that Christ did it, for, unlike Christ, he does not have power over death. He is doomed to die. But Christ spoke of his life as something that he was "giving" away, giving to his Father as a ransom for the sins of many.

St. John presents Christ as foreseeing his passion and walking determinedly toward it. After the Last Supper, when the soldiers and court attendants came out to the Garden to arrest him, he revealed his power over his assailants by terrifying them with his word alone. "When Jesus said, 'I am he,' they moved back and fell to the ground" (John 18:6). Moments later, after Peter had struck off the right ear of Malchus, Christ told them that it was within his power to summon more than twelve legions of angels to his defense—once again indicating that he entered upon his passion voluntarily. He stayed his hand and refused to undo the powers that were uniting against him. He let them lead him away, scourge him, beat him, crown him with thorns; finally, he offered them his arms and legs that they might drive nails into them.

Just before Christ gave up his spirit, he uttered a loud cry. "And when Jesus had cried out in a loud voice, he said, 'Father, into your hands I commend my spirit.' With these words he breathed his last" (Luke 23:46). For a man at the point of death this was a remarkable act. It indicated that reserves of strength were still available to him. For after protracted suffering most men are eventually reduced to a scarcely audible whisper, and they die weakly. But with Jesus it was otherwise. Death did not come upon him as a thief. He opened the door to it. Freely he let death seize him. Like a warrior who suddenly exposes himself to the onthrust of his adversary, Christ allowed death to kill him. It was a surrender he did not have to make, a gift he did not have to give.

It might be objected that Christ's action upon Calvary was not really so unique, and that many martyrs and soldiers have met their end with equivalent valor. Numerous instances could be cited of men who laid down their lives voluntarily, who freely exposed themselves to inevitable death, a death, moreover, that they could have avoided.

Without minimizing the nobility of such actions, there is one fundamental difference between what they did and what Christ did. Sooner or later, the martyr and the soldier must inevitably die. Being descendants of Adam, they bear within themselves the seed of sin, and therefore the seed of their own eventual demise. But sin did not touch Christ, and therefore death had no power over him. Christ was mortal only because he willed to be so. His death was altogether voluntary.

Many causes concurred to bring about Christ's passion and death. The Father himself was involved. The Father, along with Mary, supplied the "matter" of the sacrifice—Christ's physical humanity. And not only that, the Father inspired Christ's will with the desire to offer up his life in this way. He moved Christ to make this offering. Thus, this was not merely Christ's sacrifice; it was the Father's as well. He was acting with and in his Son. He was sacrificing his Son for the sake of men. In a way, he did to his Son, Jesus, what Abraham almost did to his son, Isaac.

Christ was both the priest and the victim of this action: he offered, he was offered. His offering consisted in his manifest willingness to undergo the passion for the specific purpose of worshiping God in such a way that men would be redeemed. On the other hand, his victimhood consisted in everything that happened to his visible, mortal body from the moment of his capture till the moment of his death. Traditionally the separation of his body and blood on the cross has been regarded as the sign *par excellence* of his victimhood.

According to the Jewish concept of sacrifice, once the victim had been given to God it belonged to him, and was thereby divinized. Contact with a sacrificed victim brought one into some kind of contact with God himself. This was the idea behind the Hebrew communion sacrifices. In eating the victim they were eating "divine food."

Something analogous, yet far more transcendent, occurred at Christ's death. Christ was mankind's offering to God; he was mankind's victim. Once that victim had been given to God, any man who made contact with it (through faith or the sacraments of faith) would thereby contact God himself. At the moment of his death, Christ's humanity, the material of his sacrifice, became the one and only means through which men could contact God. Before his death, Christ had been the moral Head of mankind, with the right to act in the name of all. He had also been Head in dignity, and all men owed their reverence and submission to him. But only at his death did his actual humanity become the source of divine life for all men.

Calvary was not simply the sacrifice of one man. It was a collective action. It was offered through one man and by one man, but for an entire race. In offering himself Christ was offering all humanity. Every prayer and supplication, every suffering endured, every virtuous action performed by any member of the human race was offered to God by Christ on Calvary. Therefore, just as the human race can point to only one priest—Jesus Christ, so also it knows but one saving sacrifice —the sacrifice of the cross. There is no other way for men to come to God except through the cross of Jesus.

It is not difficult for the believer to see that on Calvary Christ was offering a sacrifice. But how does he know that this sacrifice was accepted by God?

Strictly speaking, he does not "know" this. He believes it. But here faith is not without its support. There are reasons why Christ's sacrifice should have been, and was in fact accepted by the Father. As has already been mentioned, the Father himself was involved in this sacrifice. The Father sent his Son to offer it; he gave him the body that was offered; he inspired him with the will to make the offering. Since, therefore, the Father took part in the offering, it is hardly likely that He should have refused it.

But perhaps the surest indication that God accepted Christ's offering was the Resurrection. In raising Christ from the dead and having him appear before men, the Father was signaling his acceptance of Christ's saving work. Through his human powers alone, Christ could never have risen. This was a divine work. It was God's way of telling the world that the man Jesus was all that he claimed to be and that his sacrifice was truly the source of salvation for men.

3. The Last Supper

The first Mass was most probably celebrated in the course of a Jewish paschal meal. This was the annual commemoration of the meal that the Hebrews had eaten hastily, with staffs in their hands and dressed for their journey, on the night of their Exodus from Egypt. At that meal each Hebrew family had sacrificed a lamb and sprinkled its blood on the doors of their houses so that the angel of destruction would "pass-over" their dwellings and not kill the first-born children within. Shortly after eating the lamb they began their journey into the Promised Land.

In Christ's time this meal was eaten joyfully yet solemnly. The participants reclined upon cushions strewn about the floor.

It began with two blessings: a blessing of the feast itself and then of the wine that was to be served. Then all the guests washed their right hands and ate a course of bitter herbs, dipping them into a salted sauce. This was meant to remind them of their bitter years of slavery.

Before the meal itself could begin, the father of the family reminded his household of the significance of the feast and its various dishes. The unleavened bread, he said, was a reminder of the bread that did not have time to rise on the night of the first pasch. The lamb was a symbol of those lambs whose blood had stayed the hand of the destroying angel. The wine was a token of the joy and gratitude they experienced in recalling God's interventions in their behalf. After this the family recited the first part of the *Hallel,* a hymn consisting of Psalms 113 to 118, and then they shared a cup of wine.

Finally, after they had washed both hands, the main part of the meal began, the part in which the paschal lamb and the unleavened bread were eaten. This central action of the feast was framed by two blessings: at the beginning the bread was blessed, and at the end a cup of wine.

According to Père Benoit, it seems likely that these two blessings were altered by Christ so as to constitute a "new pasch." Thus, after the first part of the Hallel and after the washing of their hands, Christ would have blessed the bread, broken it, and distributed it to his disciples, saying, "This is my body, which will be given for you; do this as a memorial of me" (Luke 22:19). Then, after having eaten the lamb, Jesus would have taken a cup of wine and passed it to them saying, "Drink all of you from this, for this is my blood, the blood of the covenant, which is to be poured out for many for the forgiveness of sins" (Matt. 26:27).

The fact that Jesus inaugurated this rite in the course of a paschal meal was of profound symbolic significance. To St. John the paschal lamb was a figure of Christ. Christ was the lamb, the lamb that was slain, the lamb who takes away the sins of the world. By the sacrifice of this lamb a new people of God were freed from the slavery of sin. A pilgrim people began its march to a new promised land. God would spare all who had washed themselves in the blood of the lamb. And just as the first Jewish pasch anticipated the covenant made on Sinai, so now this pasch preceded the covenant that was to be sealed on Calvary.

For the past several centuries theologians have been trying to gain a deeper understanding of the relations between what happened in the Upper Room and what happened at Calvary.

The Council of Trent taught that at the Last Supper Christ "offered his body and blood under the species of bread and wine to God the Father," and that he did this "in order that he might leave to his beloved spouse, the Church . . . , a visible sacrifice by which that bloody sacrifice which was to be performed once upon the cross would be represented, and its memory remain until the end of the world, and its salutary efficacy be applied for the forgiveness of those sins we daily commit." [10] Two points here are particularly significant: first, that the Last Supper was itself a true sacrifice, "a visible sacrifice"; second, that its foremost purposes were (a) to memorialize Christ's death on the cross by re-presenting it, and (b) to communicate the redemptive efficacy of Christ's sacrifice to men.

In several respects the Last Supper and Calvary were identical. First of all, the same external reality was offered to God at the Last Supper as was offered to God on the cross—namely, the body and blood of Christ. Secondly, the same priest who made the offering on Calvary also made the offering in the Cenacle. Thus, both sacrifices have the same priest and the same victim. Thirdly, the ultimate purpose of each was the same. Both were ordered to God's glory through the salvation of men.

Nor is this all. For in one sense the Last Supper and Calvary were only one action. We have here one internal sacrifice, one spiritual sacrifice, which was given two distinct external expressions. In the Cenacle Christ expressed this offering sacramentally; on the cross he expressed it physically.

Christ's "hour," the climactic act of his life, did not consist solely in the time he spent on the cross. It lasted from Thursday evening until the moment of his death. When this "hour" began, Christ commenced a single internal offering that was not complete until he died. "It was before the festival of the Passover, and Jesus knew that *the hour had come* for him to pass from this world . . ." (John 13:1; emphasis added). The Last Supper and Calvary constituted a single spiritual sacrifice offered in two distinct ways. On the cross he offered it physically or naturally; in the Cenacle he offered it sacramentally.

So, first, we have the fact that these two external offerings were but different signs of one and the same internal offering. Second, we can say that the sign confected in the Cenacle was itself a sign of Calvary. Thus, whereas the offering made on Calvary was only a sign of Christ's interior, spiritual sacrifice, the offering made in the Upper Room was both a sign of Calvary and a sign of the interior offering underlying Calvary. Or, to put it more simply, the Supper signified the totality of Calvary, both in its internal and external aspects. This being so, the new rite took its entire being and meaning from the reality which it imaged. The new rite was instituted so that men might commemorate Calvary and unite themselves to Christ in his sanctifying worship of the Father.

Having seen the relation between the Supper and Calvary, we now turn to the relation between Christ's "hour" and the Masses celebrated each day. First, they are related as a deed commanded is related to the command itself. Every Mass is celebrated out of obedience to Christ's precept, "Do this in remembrance of me." Second, they are related as a sign is related to the thing it signifies. The Mass, with its separate consecration, is a sign and symbol of Christ's death. Third, they are related as a source of power is related to that which communicates power. The Mass communicates the redemptive power of Calvary.

We said above that the Last Supper and Calvary were different embodiments of a single internal action. This is not true, however, of the relation between the Last Supper and Calvary, on the one hand, and the Masses that are celebrated today, on the other.

The offering that Christ makes at Mass is a numerically different action, internally and externally, from the one he made on Calvary. The sacrifice of the Mass does not repeat or continue the sacrifice of Calvary. As a unique historical event, Calvary has ceased to be and is incapable of being repeated. "He sits forever at the right hand of God, after offering a sacrifice for our sins that is *never repeated*" (Heb. 10:12). The Epistle to the Hebrews insists that redemption came through one offering, and one offering only. In accordance with the divine will we have been sanctified "by the *offering* of his *body* made once and for all by Jesus Christ" (10:10). And again, "By virtue of that one single offering, he has achieved the eternal perfection of all whom he is sanctifying" (10:14).

What, then, is the function of the Mass? Christ uses it to re-state his offering, to point to it, to re-present it to God as *the* manifestation of his worship of him. As Father Kiesling puts it: "He offers now his sacrificial-offering-then." [11] In the Mass Christ is, as it were, saying to the Father: "That which I offered once on Calvary, *that* is my offering, my one offering, which now I reaffirm and ratify. Accept and sanctify those who are now sacramentally re-enacting it, as you accepted and glorified me when I offered it on the cross."

The Mass is a sacramental sacrifice. But this does not render it false or unreal. It remains a true sacrifice, but a commemorative one. It is not a re-actualization of Calvary, not a repetition of it, nor even a continuation of it. It is an "image" of it, a sacramental image, an image that contains the reality it images, contains it really, but mysteriously. In the Mass the sacrifice of Calvary is *present* . . . sacramentally. How? We do not know. We believe.

Finally, we cannot separate this sacrifice from the sacramental meal that completes it. In eating the sacrificed body and blood of Christ men both express and effect their desire to become one with him, to be identified with him as a victim totally given over to the Father. In receiving the Eucharist, said Augustine, "It is not Christ who is changed into us; it is we who are changed into Christ." Furthermore, in eating this victim we also declare and deepen our intention to live in peace and love with all those who share the Lord's table. The Eucharist is the sacrament of Christian unity—unity with God and with men, in Christ.

The whole Mass from beginning to end is an expression of Christ's love, an expression of his desire to be present with men till the end of time, an expression of his everlasting desire for the welfare of his human brothers. Through it he gives men the opportunity to join him in his worship of the Father and so to be ever more profoundly incorporated into his body. And through the Eucharist he has given men all that he could give them. He has given them himself.

D. THE PRIESTHOOD OF CHRIST IN HEAVEN

1. *The Effect of Christ's Death Upon His Priesthood*

The moment of a man's death is, in one sense, a moment that will last forever. For the basic state of a man's soul when death overtakes him will perdure forever. The soul that dies hating God will hate him forever; and the soul that dies loving him will love him forever. Even the intensity of one's love or hate will be fixed. After a man experiences death, he no longer has the power either to improve or diminish himself. There are no "opportunities" in heaven. The nobility of soul, or lack thereof, that a man possesses at death will be his portion forever. In this regard, the ancient proverb, "As a man lives, so shall he die," might well be switched around. "As a man dies, so shall he live . . . forever."

Thus it is with every man, and thus it was with Christ. When with a loud cry he gave up the ghost and thereby drank the last dregs of the chalice his Father had prepared for him, he "passed over" to a new kind of existence. This was his *exodus* —an exodus compared to which its analogue in Jewish history was only a faint shadow.

Under Moses and Joshua a people had passed out of slavery into a land of promise. Now, Jesus was passing out of a world of slavery, out of a world enmeshed in the slavery of sin, and passing into a world of life and purity and spiritual freedom. Unlike that earlier exodus that had lasted forty years, this new exodus was effected in a moment of time. At one moment Christ was experiencing man's ultimate defeat; at the next, he was experiencing the beginning of his heavenly exaltation. What accrued to him in that moment of transition was destined to belong to him forever. He was entering into his eternal inheritance.

For Christ this involved more than for an ordinary man, and this not simply because Christ was holier than others, but more precisely because the Father had authorized him to act as mankind's high priest. This meant that everything that Christ experienced had reverberations upon the whole human race. It meant that his death, inasmuch as it was a sacrificial act undergone in behalf of all men, implicated every human being. His death was the *Kairos*, the time, the culminating moment of all history, the moment in which mankind, in and through its high priest, was released from its bondage to the prince of this world and restored to the grace and love of God.

When Christ died, one stage of his priestly work came to an end. But no sooner did that first stage end than a second began. The first stage had been marked by trial and tragedy; the cross was its symbol. The second stage would be marked by power and glory; a crown was its symbol. The first had underlined man's weakness; the second would focus upon God's power. And yet between these two stages there was an intimate relation. For Christ, at the hour of his greatest weakness, uttered the human appeal that brought into being the drama of God's power.

When Christ emptied himself to the ultimate, God entered to fill that emptiness. Everything that happened to Christ after he gave up his spirit to God—his resurrection, ascension, glorification—and everything that would ever be accomplished through him for all eternity was pre-caused and pre-contained in that moment when God accepted his spirit. Every gift of the Spirit that men would subsequently receive was then and there obtained by Christ. All that remained was for time to run its course and for Christ to communicate to individual men the grace that Calvary had brought him.

At the moment of his Passover Christ's priesthood was invested with a fullness of power that had not previously been his. At that moment he was made the *Kyrios,* the Lord of history and creation. At that moment he became a *royal priest,* a priest-king, a priest empowered to confer salvation upon all who united themselves to him. Not that royalty and power were not his before, but that in the design of God he was not meant to enter into the fullness of his royal priesthood until after his death.

The Epistle to the Hebrews says that Christ's priesthood was perfected by what he underwent upon the cross, and that his ministry became more universal, more powerful, and more beneficial to men than it had been before. "Although he was Son, he *learnt* to obey through suffering; but having been *made perfect,* he *became* for all who obey him the source of eternal salvation . . ." (Heb. 5:8–9; emphasis added).

Christ himself spoke of his death as a necessary precondition for the completion of his saving work. "Unless a wheat grain falls on the ground and dies, it remains only a single grain; but if it dies, it yields a rich harvest" (John 12:24). Similarly: "And when I am lifted up from the earth, I shall draw all men to myself" (John 12:32). And again: "It is for your own good that I am going because unless I go, the Advocate will not come to you; but if I do go, I will send him to you" (John 16:7).

Christ's sacrificial death brought his ministry into a new and more exalted region of influence. Moreover, he began to exercise this new fullness when, descending into hell, he announced salvation and conferred it upon the holy souls awaiting him there.

2. *The Meaning of the Resurrection vis-à-vis Christ's Priesthood*

The resurrection confirmed and ratified Christ's priesthood. Through this means God was signifying to men that Christ was truly their high priest, and that he and he alone could unite them to God himself. So important is the resurrection to Christ's priesthood that in the past there were some (the Socinians) who went so far as to say that Christ did not even become a priest until he rose from the dead. They held that only then did God endow Christ with priestly power and authority. This, of course, was an exaggeration. Christ was a priest throughout his life, and pre-eminently on Calvary. Nevertheless, the resurrection did effect a tremendous change in the way in which Christ could exercise his priesthood.

The life that Jesus received on the first Easter Sunday was not the same as the life he had laid down on the previous

Friday. In this the resurrection of Christ was markedly different from that of Lazarus or the son of the widow of Naim. These two were restored to their mortal lives. They returned to "life in the flesh," life as we experience it, life bound up with spiritual and physical death. But Christ rose to a new kind of life, "life in the Spirit," life freed from the impinging factors of human existence.

The risen Christ no longer depended upon food and drink, nor was he subject to fatigue or anxiety, or bound by the ordinary laws of space and time. All of the difficulties tied up with existence in the flesh were done away with. He had become a "new creature," the first-born of a new creation. All that was mortal in him was swallowed up by life, and all that was corruptible in him was made incorruptible.

When Jesus received this new life his humanity was established as the vehicle or instrument or channel through which this life would be infused into all who would come to believe in his name. Henceforth, divine life would come to human beings in and through the humanity of Jesus Christ. The Father's saving action would be done "in Christ." Grace itself became "Christian grace," being modalized by the action of Christ in transmitting it to men.

It is true, of course, that grace was "Christian" before Christ came on earth. It was "Christian" in the sense that men received it by reason of the foreseen merits of Christ. Nevertheless, the graces that saved Abraham, Isaac, and Jacob were not Christian to the same extent as are the graces that men today receive. They could not be. For they could not have been communicated through the action of Christ's human nature. That nature did not yet exist.

On the other hand, the graces conferred by Christ during his public ministry (as when he forgave the sins of the paralytic) were truly mediated through his human intellect and will. But while he remained on earth he could do this only in a limited way, for his actions, for the most part, were still hedged by the laws of space and time. His priestly ministry had not yet become universal in scope. The graces that he then mediated were portents of what would happen in a much more all-embracing way after his death. After his death he was empowered to communicate the Spirit to all men of all time; his bodily humanity became the life source for his universal community-body, the Church.

At the Resurrection Christ's body became the Temple of the universe, the one and only place where all men could encounter God. Thenceforth whoever entered this Temple entered into the presence of God. Whoever entered into it was made part of it, a "living stone" of it. "Be living stones making a spiritual house" (I Peter 2:5). Within this Temple they could offer authentic and acceptable worship to God. Within it they could obtain forgiveness for their sins and the gift of eternal life. Christ spoke of his body in this way when he said: "Destroy this sanctuary, and in three days I will raise it up" (John 2:19).

Several of the Fathers of the Church compared Christ's new risen life to the fire from heaven that consumed Elijah's sacrifice upon Mount Carmel. That fire had been God's means of signaling his acceptance of Isaiah's offering. So now figure gave way to reality, and a new type of fire, the fire of the Holy Spirit, descended upon Christ's sacrifice and consumed it. This fire devoured Christ's mortality, transforming his death from apparent defeat into victory. And so completely did this fire take hold of Christ that henceforth anyone who touched him through faith would himself be ignited.

The Fathers also used a sacrificial analogy to show the significance of Christ's ascension. They likened it to the entrance of the Aaronic high priest into the Holy of Holies, that most sacred enclosure of the Temple in which was housed the Ark of the Covenant and the two Golden Cherubim. (Together, these two objects were regarded as the throne of Yahweh, and the Jews believed that God was present there in some mysterious way.)

Once each year, on the Day of Atonement (Yom Kippur), after sacrificing a bull for his own sins and those of his household, the high priest entered this most sacred of areas. Upon entering, he said no special prayers. He merely presented some of the bull's blood to God, sprinkling it upon the golden plate atop the Ark. When this was done, the priest returned to the people and then sacrificed a goat for the sins of the whole nation, repeating the same blood-rite as before.

Christ, in the fullness of time, fulfilled this figure by bringing his own immolated body into the true Holy of Holies, into the "greater, the more perfect tent, which is better than the one made by men's hands because it is not of this created order" (Heb. 9:11). There he stands before the Father as the embodiment of humanity's longing for union with God. The Father, in beholding and accepting Christ, beholds and accepts in principle Christ's brethren. For Christ, like the Israelite high priest, entered the Holy of Holies not as a private person but as the authorized representative of a community. In opening the gates of heaven for Christ, the Father was opening them for a community. Christ entered heaven not as a lone refugee from earth but as the leader of an immense pilgrimage, and as one whose entry has secured the entrance of an endless multitude.

When he entered heaven there was effected in Christ's humanity that ultimate glorification of which the Transfiguration was a foreshadowing. In heaven Christ's priesthood and victimhood attained their ultimate fulfillment. His victimhood, far from ending at his death, was meant to endure forever. Not that he continues to suffer or that he dies again. But that he remains forever mankind's sacrificial offering to God, man's victim. And in virtue of his heavenly glorification he has become an accepted victim, a consecrated victim, a victim that God has taken possession of. In the Book of Revelation St. John continually

envisions Jesus as "the Lamb," "the Lamb who was immolated," "the Lamb who was slain." The blood of this Lamb
has taken away the sins of the world.

If Christ's victimhood achieved its ultimate fulfillment
through his heavenly glorification, so too did his priesthood.
His heavenly enthronement, of which St. John speaks, is the
scriptural symbol for the plenipotentiary powers that God then
conferred upon him. The royalty and glory of Christ's priesthood received its ultimate increment. He "sits at the right hand
of the Father"—a sign of his power and pre-eminence, a way of
saying that his will is backed by divine efficaciousness. The will
of our heavenly high priest has become the law of the kingdom
of God. St. Paul's consciousness of the power that Christ now
enjoys filled him with confidence and joy, and led him to say,
triumphantly, "He not only died for us—he rose from the dead,
and there at God's right hand he stands and pleads for us"
(Rom. 8:34).

3. Christ's Ministry in Heaven

The ministry that Christ now exercises in heaven is not simply
an ornamental "extra" added to a mission that was essentially
earthly. The sacerdotal work that Christ was commissioned to
do at his birth was meant to continue until the end of time.
In heaven Christ remains duty-bound to perfect and complete
the work that he began here on earth. He remains humanity's
high priest, and as such he has responsibilities to both God and
man. Were he, hypothetically speaking, to abandon his priestly
work, he would be failing God and failing men. This, however,
does not mean that Christ's heavenly existence is wearying and
burdensome. On the contrary, in reuniting his brothers with
his Father he finds joy and contentment.

Jesus' heavenly ministry is characterized by those same human endowments that fitted him so perfectly for his ministry
on earth. He retains in heaven that same sympathy and com-

passion that made him so approachable, and he is still as straightforward and unambiguous as he was then. Furthermore, he brings to heaven an experiential knowledge of human weakness. He knows what it means to be tempted, to be in pain, to be rejected, slandered, disbelieved. His experiential knowledge of these things refined his human sensitivity and enlarged his capacity for compassion and sympathy. For only those human beings who have actually experienced suffering and temptation are fully capable of entering into the hearts and souls of those whose minds and bodies are wracked with pain and suffering.

The primary concern of Christ's heavenly ministry, like that of his earthly ministry, is the salvation of men. Jesus is still the "Savior." In heaven he is not doing anything radically different from what he did on earth. Rather, he is completing and bringing to perfection what he started here.

The same goals that motivated him during his thirty-odd years on earth—the establishment of the kingdom of God, the transmission of the Gospel, the infusion of divine love into the human heart—continue to motivate him in heaven. What is more, all of them still fall under that one great imperative that governed Christ's every activity on earth—the fulfillment of his Father's will. Jesus still says, "My food is to do the will of the one who sent me, to complete his work" (John 4:34). In this sense, Christ's life is still totally sacrificial. Everything that he does, he does for his Father.

As for what Christ is actually doing in heaven, Sacred Scripture says relatively little, but what it does say contains a depth of implication that no human intellect will ever fully comprehend. It says, first of all, that Christ is in heaven as our "advocate." John writes: "We have our advocate with the Father, Jesus Christ, who is just" (I John 2:1). An advocate is one who intercedes in behalf of another. This same truth is stated in Hebrews, where Christ is said to be continually praying for men. "His power to save is utterly certain, since he is living for ever to intercede for all who come to God through him" (Heb. 7:25).

Moreover, Christ's presence in heaven is a "cause" of salvation. "Having been made perfect, he became for all who obey him the source of eternal salvation" (Heb. 5:9). Christ himself said that once he was in heaven he would prepare a place for us, and that he would send us the Spirit. Also, he promised that he would be with us all days, even till the end of the world; that he would be in our midst when we pray together; and that he would speak to us through the Apostles and their successors. "Anyone who listens to you listens to me" (Luke 10:16).

In their attempts to describe exactly what Christ is doing in heaven the Fathers of the Church do not manifest universal agreement. There are some who maintain that Christ exercises his heavenly ministry simply by being present in the true Holy of Holies. They point out that on the Day of Atonement the high priest of the Old Law entered into the Holy of Holies, not saying any prayers but simply bearing with him the sacrificial blood, which was itself a plea for divine mercy and forgiveness. So now, they say, Christ's mere presence in heaven is a prayer that moves God to save those whom he represents. As Gregory the Great states, "He 'speaks' to the Father for us in that he presents himself to the Father in our likeness. His words, his petitions consist precisely in this: He presents himself to the Father as man for mankind." [12]

But to conceive of Christ's heavenly ministry in this way is to dehumanize and deactivate it; it is to forget that in heaven Christ continues to be a man and, as such, continues to have an obligation to worship God and assist men with his whole being—with his intellect and will, with his emotions, with his body. Christ is more than a mere presence in heaven. He is a human being with a work that he must complete in a human way. The fact that Christ's body is glorified makes him more human, not less so. It does not transform him into an angel.

His emotional and bodily life, his intellectual activity, are not obliterated but perfected, glorified.

Therefore, when the Epistle to the Hebrews says that Christ "intercedes" for us, we need not understand this as some sort of metaphor. No, Christ is actually praying in heaven. He petitions, adores, gives thanks, praises. In serving as our advocate he is pleading with God to have mercy on us.

Nor are these prayers impersonal and objective pleas for mankind in general. They are the prayers of a first-born son to his Father for his many brothers. They are the prayers of one who has a personal knowledge and personal love for each and every man. They are singularly efficacious prayers inasmuch as they all originate "in the Spirit." Christ's intellectual and affective faculties are so responsive to the impulses of the Holy Spirit, so utterly attuned to divine Providence, that his prayers are but a human expression of the divine Will. God's will and Christ's are in perfect accord.

Christ's earthly and heavenly ministries are profoundly interconnected. Everything that Christ does now derives its effectiveness from what he did then. By divine decree, redemption came through Christ's pasch. That action and no other contains man's salvation. Christ, therefore, does not offer new sacrifices in heaven. Nor does he base his prayers for us upon what he is doing now, but rather upon that one work that consummated his mortal life.

In heaven Christ's prayer to the Father consists in reaffirming the sacrifice that he offered on Calvary, and in asking that it might become beneficial to souls here and now laboring toward union with God. This reaffirmation, this ratification, this renewal of the sacrifice he offered on Calvary is the heavenly counterpart of the Mass. By means of it he petitions the Father to effect in men that same paschal mystery that has already been effected in him.

Finally, we ask, is there a liturgy in heaven? Both the Epistle to the Hebrews and the Book of Revelation speak of heavenly rites and ceremonies. For example:

In my vision, I heard the sound of an immense number of angels gathered round the throne and the animals and the elders; there were ten thousand times ten thousand of them *and* thousands upon thousands, *shouting, 'The Lamb that was sacrificed is worthy to be given power, riches, wisdom, strength, honour, glory and blessing.'*
Then I heard all the living things in creation—everything that lives in the air, and on the ground, and under the ground, and in the sea, crying, 'To the One who is sitting on the throne and to the Lamb, be all praise, honour, glory and power, for ever and ever.'

[Rev. 5:11–13]

No one, of course, can say with certitude exactly what goes on in heaven. "Eye has not seen, nor has ear heard. . . ." It is possible that Jesus, beholding God, adores, worships, and prays without any specific external expressions. It is possible that in the New Jerusalem there are no structured manifestations of religious worship. It is possible that when faith gives way to vision, the externalities of religion will pass away and our worship will become solely a matter of the spirit.

These things are possible but they are unlikely. For it is natural that man, composed as he is of body as well as of soul, should express his internal sentiments in an external way, and it is natural that men who love one another and who share a common love and reverence for God should express themselves communally. If grace does not destroy these natural inclinations, why should glory, which is the flowering of grace, do so?

It would seem then that there may well be a true heavenly liturgy over which Christ as high priest presides. His prayer and his action would be its unifying elements. Thus, as on earth, so also in heaven, all worship would ascend to the Father through Christ, with him, and in him. This heavenly liturgy, already begun and already perfected in its high priest, would attain its ultimate perfection at the Parousia, when the full number of the elect will unite their praise and adoration to his.

This liturgy would never cease, for God will always be God, Christ will always be Christ, and men will always be men. Throughout all eternity, creatures would unite around their high priest to express their gratitude, worship, and praise, and in doing this their happiness would be complete.

But we need not wait until death and glory to participate in this heavenly liturgy. The Epistle to the Hebrews states that even now those who are united to Christ are united to him in his heavenly priesthood. With him they have already entered into the Holy of Holies. They have already passed into the presence of God. Their worship, their intercession, their praise are already heavenly. Already they share in Christ's heavenly priesthood.

4 / THE PRIESTHOOD OF CHRISTIANS

In this chapter we shall consider two closely related subjects. The first concerns the priesthood of the whole Church and those qualities that characterize its priestly existence. The second pertains specifically to the priesthood of the laity.

A. THE PRIESTHOOD OF THE CHURCH

In speaking of the priesthood of the Church we are referring to the priesthood of the whole community and of all its members, irrespective of whether they are in heaven or on earth, or of whether they are laymen or clerics. We are referring to the people as a whole, to the community as such, and not to any specific part of it. What we say here applies to and affects every Christian, be he pope, bishop, priest, or layman.

1. *The Priestly Vocation of the Church*

Our Lord's earthly work of re-creating mankind was at once both complete and incomplete. It was complete in that through it he laid the axe to the root of Satan's power over humanity. It was complete in that through his sacrifice he became the "new man" through whom a new humanity would come into being. It was complete in that he returned to heaven after paying in full the price of man's redemption. It was complete causally, but not effectually.

Like a serum that contains a cure for some disease but must be injected before it can achieve its healing work, so Christ's death and resurrection contained the cure for man's sickness of soul, but it still had to be "administered" to men before it could do them good. This incompleteness of Christ's saving work was not due to any inherent imperfection in it, but rather to God's desire that men should cooperate with him in the work of redemption. The new creation, like the old, was meant to challenge and engage men. It summoned them to be not spectators but participants.

Before ascending to heaven Christ founded a community and entrusted it to finish the work he had started. This did not mean that once Christ ascended his work ceased and that of the community began. No, it meant that the work that he had begun in his natural body he would now complete in and through his Mystical Body, the Church. His work became the community's work without for a moment ceasing to be his. "The ministry of the Church," writes T. F. Torrance, "is related to the ministry of Christ in such a way that in and through the ministry of the Church, it is always Christ himself who is at work." [13]

In founding this community, Christ did not allow it to choose its own objectives. Its vocation was to be essentially the same as his; it was to be a projection, a continuation, and an extension of his. This people was "sent" by Christ, just as Christ had been "sent" by the Father. Both were called to the same work of engendering a new humanity, united to God and united among themselves.

When Christ rose from the dead, he became the "first-born" of this new race, and was given the power to propagate it throughout the world. As Adam had been given the power to procreate human life, so now the man Christ was given the power to "procreate" divine life. On Pentecost Sunday Christ communicated this power to the Church. He empowered his followers to collaborate with him in the work of forming a new race.

The specific powers conferred upon the Church constituted a share in Christ's own priestly, prophetic, and royal power. The Church as prophet is called to reiterate to every generation and in every possible manner God's offer of salvation in Jesus Christ. The substance of this offer is a summons to take part in a historical event, Christ's hour, his passion, death, and resurrection. It is a summons to die and rise with Christ, initially through faith and baptism, and subsequently through every action of the Christian man. The Church proclaims an event, a deed. It serves notice that this event contains the cure for what separates man from himself, from other men, and from God.

Allied to and associated with her prophetic office is the Church's royal or pastoral ministry. This involves every action by which she, in and through her members, shepherds men toward ever greater union with Christ. It includes all the ways in which Christ influences men through his community. It is directed not only to those outside the fold; it is also at work within the community itself, its various members affecting one another in different ways. In this sense the Church's pastoral ministry includes and embraces her other ministries. For her prophetic and priestly actions are but two of the ways in which, through Christ, she shepherds and influences men.

Nevertheless, inasmuch as the community's ultimate goal is the communication of the grace won on Calvary, and inasmuch as she achieves this by participating in Christ's heavenly priesthood, her vocation, like Christ's, is pre-eminently a priestly one. It is centered in Christ's sacrifice. Its whole effort is aimed at involving and engaging men in Christ's sacrifice. All its activities point to and participate in a single activity—the continuing pasch of Christ's Mystical Body, the death and resurrection of Christ as it mystically recurs in Christians.

Everything subserves this one finality, and for this reason all her works are inherently sacerdotal, and her whole existence assumes a sacrificial modality. Her inner life is inspired by that same sacrificial spirit of filial self-surrender that inspired the life of Christ. All of her actions, whether they be doctrinal, juridical, or sacramental, are at bottom sacrificial. For all of them originate in filial love and obedience.

2. A Sacramental Vocation

A sacrament is a unique kind of sign. Ordinarily, signs communicate only images or ideas. We see smoke rising in the distance and we know that somewhere below it there is a fire. We see birds migrating and we know that winter is on its way. Words themselves are signs—"conventional" signs with which we learn to associate different images and concepts. But a sacrament communicates more than mere ideas or images. It speaks to the whole person; it affects the whole person, and not simply his mind. We see this from natural, human sacraments such as a particularly thoughtful gift or a beautiful expression of love.

These things move the whole man. They uplift and re-create the entire person. But to do this they must be received and recognized for what they are. Christ, for example, could not communicate sacramentally with those who were totally closed to him. For them his external actions did not communicate his internal love and power. A sacrament cannot be received *as a sacrament* unless it is received by an open person. Furthermore, the more open a person is, the more totally can he be affected by sacramental expressions. In Christianity it is faith that opens a person to Christ's sacramentality.

Christ, in his humanity, was the sacrament of God's love for man. Through his very existence as well as through his actions he expressed that love and, in expressing it, conferred and communicated it. His life, to those who saw it with the eyes of faith, was a translucent communication of divine goodness and truth. Yet his sacramentality was not static or unchanging. He did not communicate in the same way that a statue or a painting communicates, but more in the manner of a symphony or drama. His "meaning" developed and evolved. Each of the great mysteries of his life—his temptation, his baptism, the Transfiguration—added to its profundity and beauty. And just as the ultimate meaning of a play emerges only in the final scene, so Christ, as sacrament of his Father's redemptive love, was not sacramentally complete until he returned whence he came and sent forth the Spirit upon mankind.

Only then did Christ attain the fullness of his sacramentality; only then could men see in him what the author of the Epistle to the Hebrews saw: the heir of all things by whom God had made the world, the brightness of God's glory and the image of his substance; he who upholds all things by the word of his power and who, having effected man's purgation, took his seat at the right hand of God (Heb. 1:2–3).

Seen as a whole, Christ's life sacramentalized one central truth—that God in his love had wrought the salvation of men through the passion, death, and resurrection of his Son. Christ's ultimate meaning is contained in the mystery of his pasch. That event embodied the message of his whole life. It is the final explanation of everything he ever did.

Christ was "sent" to be the sacrament of his Father's love. He in turn founded a community to sacramentalize his love—to express and communicate that love down through history. The Church, writes Father McCabe, "is Christ existing sacramentally in the world." [14]

In order to actualize its sacramentality the Church must conform itself to Christ, as Christ conformed himself to the Father. This entails, first of all, *interior* conformity so that the mind and soul of Christ become the mind and soul of the Church, and so that the Church aspires to no other goal but that aspired to by Christ. The assimilation and retention of such a spirit requires that the Church understand itself in the same way as Christ understood himself—as son and servant, as one sent forth on a mission of salvation.

Secondly, the Church must be *externally* conformed to Christ. Otherwise men will not see in the community a reflection of its founder. In fact the Church's internal conformity to Christ does not become sacramental until it receives visible, external expression. Everything about this community—its organization, its works, its style of life, its customs, its laws, and especially its members themselves—is meant to be sacramental. Everything about it is meant to reveal and communicate its inner life. In sacramentalizing its interior spirit, Christ is, as it were, reincarnated, and through this mystical incarnation he continues his saving work.

Whereas Christ was always the perfect sacrament of the Father (that is, a perfect revelation of the Father, a perfect instrument through which he could communicate his love), the sacramentality of the Church is not so perfect. The reason for this is that in every heart, no matter how holy, there is a force that works to disfigure the Body of Christ, a force that accounts for the proverb that "Christians are ordinary people who make extraordinary claims." Every member of the Church, although he is a sacramental person empowered to reveal and communicate Christ to men, is also a sinner and thus can choose to sacramentalize the devil, to reveal and communicate the power of the "prince of this world."

We have Christ's word for it that his community will always remain substantially faithful to him. "So I now say to you: You are Peter and on this rock I will build my Church. And the gates of the underworld can never hold out against it" (Matt. 16:18). Nevertheless, during its progress through history, the sacramentality of this community will always be limited. It will always be partially disfigured by the sinfulness of its own members. Only on the Last Day, when it will finally be wholly loosed from the strictures of sin, will it perfectly recapitulate Christ in its inward and outward being. Only then will the new humanity be the perfect corporate image of the new man.

3. A Eucharistic Community

If the Church fulfills its calling by giving sacramental expression to God's saving love for men in Christ, nowhere is its sacramentality so perfectly realized as in the Eucharist, the focal communal act of the Church. The Eucharist sacramentalizes the Church's present, its past, and its future.

The Church as a *present* reality is a communion of life; it is the community of those who have passed from death to life; it is a community of adopted sons sharing in the life of a common Father. The Mass sacramentalizes this unity. It both reveals and actualizes it. The congregation converges around its priest or bishop. There they make common confession of their sinfulness (Confiteor); there they beg God's mercy (Kyrie), praise his goodness (Gloria), and beg his favor (Prayer). Together they listen to his word (Lesson and Gospel) and then assent to the truth of that word (Creed). Together they offer themselves to the Father (Offertory), an offering that Christ makes his own (Consecration). Finally, through their sharing of the Lord's Supper they give ultimate expression to their union with one another in Christ.

The Church has always been aware of the relation existing between Christ's Eucharistic Body and his Mystical Body. The one causes the other. On the one hand, Christ acting through his Mystical Body brings his Eucharistic Body into being; on the other, Christ acting through his Eucharistic Body conserves and fosters his Mystical Body, the "total Christ." St. John Chrysostom, speaking of the Eucharist, said that it "makes us his Body not only by faith, but in very truth. . . . We *become* the Body which we receive." [15] Moreover, when a person receives the body and blood of Our Lord, he is not only drawn into closer union with Christ; he is also more closely united to the whole community. As Canon Mura states: "To commune with Christ is to commune with the Church; it is to be united through Christ to all the members of the Mystical Body in the measure that they are united to the head." [16]

The Church as a reality rooted in the *past* is the community brought into being through a decisive historical event—Christ's pasch. The Eucharist makes that event present, not only symbolically but actually as well—actually yet sacramentally. There is at Mass the same priest, the same victim, and the same specific offering as there was on Calvary; but they are all there in a different way, a sacramental way. The Mass is a sacramental re-enactment of the sacrifice of Calvary.

Therefore the sacrifice of the Mass and the sacrifice of the cross are not two sacrifices. They are one and the same sacrifice present in two different ways. Furthermore, the Mass exists for the same ultimate purpose as Calvary—the purpose of uniting men with God. Christ's offering on the cross radically achieved man's redemption and reconciliation. Because of that one offering, redemption and reconciliation are now realities. Christ's offering at Mass enables men to unite their self-offering to his definitive offering, and thereby to die and rise with him. The Mass unites us to the risen Christ to the extent that we unite ourselves to the dying Christ.

As a reality looking forward to the *future* the Church longs for the day of its final purgation and divinization. Not only does it await that day; it also strives toward it, seeking always to advance from the Alpha which is Christ to the Omega which is Christ recapitulated. The Mass, with its prayers reaching out to all the members of Christ's Body in heaven, in purgatory, and on earth, draws men's minds to that ultimate consummation. It unites men spiritually to the whole of which they are parts, and in appreciating this union there is hope and strength and joy.

But the Mass does even more than this. It not only focuses our attention upon what we are and what we will be. It also actually brings the community closer to its final destiny. It prepares the world for that culminating event that will result in a new heaven and a new earth. It builds up the Body of Christ, and extends and deepens Christ's hold on creation; it hastens the day when he will be all in all. The individual Christian, through his participation in the Eucharist, is himself taking part in laying the foundations for the eschatalogical kingdom of God. He is constructing the New Jerusalem.

The centrality of the Eucharist in Christian life highlights the centrality of its sacerdotal ministry. For, just as Christ's life centered upon his "hour," so also the life of the Church is centered upon the sacramental re-presentation of that hour. And just as everything that Christ did on earth was either a preparation for or a consequence of his sacrifice, so also everything that he does now through the Church is either a preparation for or a consequence of his sacramental sacrifice.

4. The Community of the Cross

Because the Church is meant to be the "imago Christi," as Adam was called to be the "imago Dei," the function of the cross in the life of Christ contains an ocean of significance for the life of Christ's Body, the Church. The Church has drawn all of its life from the death of Christ. It *exists* to the extent that the crucified and risen Christ exists in it. It can actively enter into his redemptive work only to the degree that it has undergone Calvary. For the individual Christian this means that he can personally forward Christ's work only if he is carrying his cross. As Father de Lubac has written, "The same holds true of the Church in her members as of the Church in her

Head: she can redeem with him only as she was redeemed by Him—on the cross." [17]

In Christianity there are not many crosses; there is only one —the cross of Christ; there are not many sacrifices, but only one—the sacrifice of Christ. The world has not been saved by the sum significance of many deaths, but by one death encompassing all deaths. The Christian is a person who has undergone Christ's death. Christ's own death has occurred in him, has happened to him. Thus, he had died the death that was the death of death.

The Christian is dead and risen, and yet neither his death nor his resurrection is complete. Nor will it be complete until the last vestige of the old man has been destroyed. Till then he lives under a continual death sentence; till then he must die daily, gradually overcoming the resistance of his own being to the undisputed hegemony of Christ. The last battle of this war ends with man's physical destruction. But here the Christian, like Christ, overcomes in being overcome and conquers in being conquered. Here, if man lets him, God reaches down into a man's being and uproots the evil that man himself cannot get at. Here God takes hold of a man, as he took hold of Christ, and turns his suffering into a source of grace and future glory.

But the cross remains a scandal, and suffering continues to be a mystery. It is as hard to accept as it always was; yet through faith we know that by reason of Christ's sufferings, our own sufferings have acquired redemptive value. Nothing in life need be wasted. As Paul wrote to the Romans, "For those who love God, everything conspires for good" (Rom. 8:28). Thus it is that in the Morning Offering we offer to God as a spiritual sacrifice all our "prayers, works, and sufferings" for the salvation of all men.

Does this mean that Christian spirituality consists in supine surrender to all manner of suffering? Is the true Christian the one who awaits evil and the evil day with a kind of supernatural masochism? No, God's will is for life, not death, for happiness, not for suffering. We act as God would have us act when we struggle against evil and reduce to a minimum the sufferings which assault humanity from every side. The more we work to repel human suffering, the more closely do we cleave to the heart and action of God.

The true Christian is one who enters the lists against evil and boldly endeavors to unhorse it, while, at the same time, at the bottom of his heart there is an anticipatory tendency to acceptance and final resignation, a readiness to accept what cannot be overcome. This is one aspect of Christian humility —the realization that God can use evil itself to overthrow evil, and that the ultimate victory is in his hands, not ours.

B. THE PRIESTHOOD OF THE LAITY

We have now arrived at the very heart of our subject—the priesthood possessed by the lay Christian. This we shall consider from two distinct angles. First, we shall present the history or evolution of this doctrine. Secondly, we shall attempt to synthesize the doctrine under several headings.

1. From New Testament Times to Vatican II

Sacred Scripture, the writings of the Fathers and Doctors of the Church, and Vatican Council decrees all testify that every Christian is a priest. Paradoxically, Scripture itself never speaks of ordained ministers as priests, but gives this title only to Christ and to Christians at large. Those whom we call priests the New Testament describes as "elders" or "overseers," men selected to lead the community in worship (particularly the Eucharist), to preach the Gospel, and to provide authoritative guidance in matters of faith and morals.

The two most important biblical texts regarding the priesthood of the laity are taken from the First Epistle of St. Peter. Speaking to converts from paganism living in various provinces of Asia Minor, he says: "Be you yourselves as living stones, built thereon into a spiritual house, a holy priesthood, to offer spiritual sacrifices acceptable to God through Jesus Christ" (I Peter 2:5; Confraternity trans.).

Note the progression: stones, house, priesthood, sacrifices. Christians are living stones, built into a spiritual house (a temple) in which as priests they offer spiritual sacrifices. Note also that this particular text does not assert that each individual Christian is a priest, but rather that the community itself is a spiritual house and a holy priesthood. St. Paul, however, in asserting that the individual Christian is a temple ("Didn't you realise that you were God's temple and that the Spirit of God was living among you?" [I Cor. 3:16]) makes it legitimate to infer that, within the temple that is himself, each Christian is a priest and has the power to offer to God "spiritual sacrifices acceptable to God through Jesus Christ."

The second text provided by St. Peter announces the same theme: "But you are *a chosen race, a royal priesthood, a consecrated nation, a people set apart* to sing the praises of God who called you out of the darkness into his wonderful light" (I Peter 2:9).

Three things are important here. First, the fact that Peter is applying to Christians exactly the same titles that Moses and Isaiah had formerly applied to Israel, thus implying that Christians are the New Israel, the successors and heirs to the promises of old. Second, there is the implicit affirmation that Christians share in all three of Christ's missions: his priesthood, his lordship, and his prophetic office. As a "royal priesthood," they are to proclaim the goodness of him who called them. Finally, the priesthood of Christians is said to be a *royal* priesthood. This is because it issues from Christ, who was at once priest and king.

The priesthood and kingship of the Christian community are participations in the priesthood and kingship of Christ.

By reason of their priesthood, Christians have access in one Spirit to the Father (Eph. 2:18). They can draw near with confidence to the throne of grace to obtain mercy and grace in time of need (Heb. 4:16). Under the Old Dispensation only the high priest, and then only once a year, was allowed to enter the Holy of Holies, the symbolic habitation of Yahweh. Now all Christians, inasmuch as they share in Christ's high priesthood, are able to enter into the true Holy of Holies, not made by men. All who are "in Christ" have direct and immediate access to God "through Christ."

According to Father Spicq, this idea that all Christians can present themselves directly to God "is nothing less than a revolution in the fundamental conception of religion." [18] Every other ancient Near-Eastern religion had divided its adherents into those who could and those who could not speak directly to God. This is one of the most overlooked aspects of the layman's participation in Christ's priesthood.

Almost all the great early Christian writers spoke explicitly about the priesthood of all believers. To mention but a few: St. Justin Martyr states that "we are the true high priestly race of God." [19] St. Irenaeus says: "All the just possess the priestly rank." [20] Origen maintains that "a priesthood is given to the whole Church of God and to all who believe." [21] St. John Chrysostom declares: "So also, you are yourself made a priest in the Laver (Baptism) . . . a priest in that you offer yourself to God." [22] To St. Jerome goes the credit for being the first author to use the phrase "lay priesthood." In his *Dialogue Against the Luciferians,* he says that no more can a bishop be deprived of his episcopal consecration than can an ordinary Christian lose his "lay priesthood."

These seemingly unpretentious texts are rich in significance. For example, St. Irenaeus' statement that "all the just" possess the priestly rank contains the implication that everyone who is in the state of grace possesses this priesthood, irrespective of whether or not he is a visible member of the Catholic Church. On the other hand, St. Justin's comment that the layman cannot lose his priesthood indicates that justifying grace is not the only source of this priesthood, for such grace can be lost, and yet the individual remains a priest.

St. Augustine made two great contributions to the development of this teaching—first, by associating it with membership in Christ's mystical body. He held that Christians were priests by reason of their incorporation into a priestly community. Membership in this community brought with it membership in Christ's priesthood. This suggestion that the very same realities that caused a man to be united to Christ (principally grace, but also the baptismal character) also united him to his priesthood. It also suggested an intimate relation between a Christian's "sonship" and his priesthood. Just as Christ's priesthood ultimately issued from the fact that he was God's well-beloved Son, so also, the priesthood of Christians is rooted in their adoptive sonship. The Christian is a priest *because* he is a son. His sonship gives him access to God and enables him to offer acceptable sacrifices.

The second major contribution of St. Augustine arose from the way in which he correlated priesthood and victimhood. For him the two were inseparable. A man participated personally in Christ's priesthood only to the extent that he participated in his victimhood. Of Christ, the Father had asked only one offering, the offering of himself; of Christians he asks no more and no less. Under the New Dispensation all true sacrifice is self-sacrifice. "You ask what you should offer," says Augustine. "Offer yourself. For what, in effect, does God seek from you but yourself?" [23]

Here, however, we should recall that just as there is in Christianity only one priesthood into which many men are incorporated, so similarly there is only one sacrifice into which all other sacrifices are integrated. Augustine speaks of Christians united to Christ as constituting the "total Christ." In the same vein, we might add that Christians with Christ constitute the "total priest," and that their sacrifices with his make up the "total sacrifice of the total Christ."

The next great forward step in the development of this doctrine came from St. Thomas Aquinas, with his idea that the sacramental characters conferred by Baptism, Confirmation, and Holy Orders were three distinct priestly consecrations, each endowing their possessors with specific priestly powers. All three, he held, were directly ordered to the performance of sacramental actions—that is, to visible actions through which Christ exercises his heavenly priesthood.

These are primarily liturgical actions—the Mass, the sacraments—but they include also many other actions through which Christ continues to exercise his ministry of reconciliation. No better summation of such actions exists than those encompassed by the spiritual and corporal works of mercy, which are enumerated in the catechism in the following order:

Corporal Works of Mercy

1. To feed the hungry
2. To give drink to the thirsty
3. To clothe the naked
4. To shelter the shelterless
5. To visit the sick
6. To ransom the captive
7. To bury the dead

Spiritual Works of Mercy

1. To instruct the ignorant
2. To counsel the doubtful

3. To admonish the sinner
4. To bear wrongs patiently
5. To forgive offenses willingly
6. To comfort the afflicted
7. To pray for the living and the dead

The three characters, in their various ways, transform our actions into sacramental actions—that is, into signs and causes of Christ's own saving work.

According to Aquinas the baptismal character was a power for reception analogous, we might say, to the eye or the ear. Without eyes a person cannot see color; without ears he cannot hear sound. Similarly, without the baptismal character a person cannot receive the subsequent sacraments as sacraments. He lacks the power to receive them. For example, were an unbaptized person to undergo the entire ritual for the reception of the sacrament of Penance, he would no more receive the actual sacrament than would the watch on his wrist or the shirt on his back. The sacramental absolution simply will not affect him.

The character that comes with Confirmation is geared more to giving than to receiving. The confirmed Christian is a man empowered to give sacramental expression to his faith—that is, to profess it in such a way that he will serve notice of the saving power and presence of Christ. He is capacitated to give signs, indeed, to be a sign, a living sign and sacrament of Christ's will for the salvation of all men.

The character conferred by the sacrament of Holy Orders endows its possessors with the power to perform certain specified actions in the name of Christ himself. This applies most especially to the celebration of the Eucharist and to the other sacraments, but it also applies (less rigorously) to preaching and guiding. The word of the preacher is in some way the word of

Christ, and the command of the bishop is the command of Christ. "He who hears you, hears me."

Not until the sixteenth century and Martin Luther did the doctrine on the priesthood of the laity become a great divisive issue. Luther's insistence upon this teaching arose from several factors, primarily his conviction that Christianity had become the privileged preserve of priests and monks, and that in large part these clerics and monks had corrupted the true meaning of Christian life. Above all, Luther wished to re-establish the fact that every individual Christian has direct access to God, and that he need not depend so heavily on the ministrations of the ordained. In this regard, his thought is faithfully echoed by the hymn "Nothing Between":

Nothing between, Lord, nothing between;
Let me thy glory see,
Draw my soul close to thee,
Then speak in love to me;
                    Nothing between.[24]

The Catholic of the present day will not argue with Luther's motives. He will agree that medieval Christendom was disproportionately a clerical establishment. He will also agree that all too often these clerics were hirelings rather than true shepherds. Moreover, with Luther he would insist that every Christian is free to approach God by himself without needing to have his prayers mediated through an ordained priest.

Nevertheless, in trying to re-establish these fundamental truths, Luther went to the opposite extreme, going so far as to deny the very existence of a ministerial priesthood. Not that he denied the existence of a pastoral ministry with a mandate from Christ to preach the Gospel; but he did deny that such men possessed a participation in Christ's priesthood over and above that of every other Christian.

Intimately connected with this (by way of cause or effect I do not know) was his teaching that the Eucharist was only a memorial of Christ's sacrifice and not an actual re-presentation of it. This being so, the minister had no more sacrificial power than did the layman. The layman was as much a priest as the ordained minister.

Nor was this the only point at which Luther broke with the traditional Catholic teaching on the priesthood of the laity. Paradoxically, he rejected as heretical the two realities that Catholics regard as the very cornerstones of the doctrine—namely, sanctifying grace and the sacramental characters.

Luther, along with the other great Reformers, did not deny what Catholics call "uncreated grace"—that is, God's saving, justifying love for men. But both he and they did deny "created grace," which is the interior transformation that is caused by God's saving love. Traditionally, Protestants have believed in *extrinsic justification*. They believe that justification means God's *acceptance* of a sinner. Catholics believe this, too, but also believe that justification involves undergoing a death to sin at the deepest level of one's being, so that the justified man is basically no longer a sinner but is holy in the Lord. This is what is meant by *intrinsic justification*.

In denying "created grace," the Reformers were denying that the Christian is intrinsically a priest. They were saying that the Christian is a priest in the same sense as he is "just"—that is, extrinsically. This error was compounded by their rejection of the sacramental characters. Luther spoke of the Catholic teaching on the characters as a "fine papistical invention." Calvin called it a fable due to the ignorance of monks. Zwingli rejected it as non-Scriptural. In so doing they dealt another blow to the richness of this mystery. Without realizing it and surely without wishing it, they impoverished the very doctrine that they wished to strengthen.

The Catholic response to Luther's teaching was mixed and

confused. Several writers, notably Gaspar Schatzgeyer, kept their theological balance and reiterated plainly and forcefully the traditional teaching. In fact Schatzgeyer actually forwarded the doctrine by his insistence on the key point that the clerical priesthood exists for the sake of the lay priesthood—first to bring it into being, and then to foster and develop it.

Moreover, he along with others pointed out that the sacrament of Baptism was a far more important and decisive event in a man's life than the sacrament of Orders. After all, a man's salvation does not depend upon his becoming an ordained priest, but it does depend upon his being baptized. "Amen, Amen, I say to you, unless a man be born again of water and the Spirit, he cannot enter the kingdom of God" (John 3:5; Confraternity trans.).

In general, however, the Catholic reaction was unfortunate. Unfortunate, not because (as is sometimes falsely alleged) pastors and theologians denied the layman's priesthood, nor even because they tended to minimize it (which many did); unfortunate rather because for the next several centuries Catholic theologians spent most of their time and effort distinguishing and relating the two priesthoods, at the expense of positively exploring their inner content. The theology of the lay priesthood became more and more a word game in which ever more subtle and careful expressions were used to describe it—allegorical, figurative, improper, common, private.

Cajetan, for example, styled it "metaphorical" and "collective." By metaphorical he meant that the lay priesthood had no properly sacrificial power; by collective, that this priesthood accrued to the community as such and not to its members individually. In both respects he was wrong. Yet, because of his influence upon subsequent theologians, he greatly weakened the pastoral impact of the doctrine. (After all, a layman of those days might have asked, what good is it to be a collective, metaphorical priest?)

Providentially the Council of Trent did not adopt Cajetan's terminology and, in fact, produced a remarkably well-balanced, incisive description of the lay priesthood:

Inasmuch as Sacred Scripture speaks of two kinds of priesthoods, one internal and one external, it will be necessary to form a distinct idea of each.

Regarding the internal priesthood, all the faithful are said to be priests once they have been washed by the saving waters of Baptism. Especially is this true of those who have the Spirit of God and who, by the help of divine grace, have been made living members of the great high priest, Jesus Christ; for enlightened by faith which is enflamed by charity, they offer up spiritual sacrifices to God on the altar of their hearts. Among such sacrifices must be reckoned every good and virtuous action done for the glory of God.[25]

From the Council of Trent until the second quarter of the twentieth century very little original work was done on the lay priesthood—or, for that matter, in any area of lay theology. There is, however, the notable exception of Matthias J. Scheeben, who was the first theologian to see a correlation between Christ's two priestly consecrations (the Hypostatic Union and sanctifying grace) and the double consecration effected by the character and grace of Baptism. Then too, during this period, it came to be generally held that the sacrament of Confirmation perfected the work done by Baptism.

In recent times up until Vatican II the two most important works on the lay priesthood were Paul Dabin's *Le Sacerdoce royal des fidèles* and Yves Congar's *Lay People in the Church.* The great merit of Father Dabin's work is that it contains practically every important statement made about the lay priesthood from the time of the Apostolic Fathers to that of Pius XII. Its weakness (if we can call it such, for one man cannot do everything) is that it is insufficiently synthetic, and in style and format would not appeal to very many laymen. Father Congar's synthesizes the research of Father Dabin and, most important of all, draws out its pastoral implications. There is no doubt that these two works, along with the encyclicals *Mediator Dei* and *Mystici Corporis,* contributed significantly to the discussions on the priesthood of the laity at the Second Vatican Council.

The Council's teaching on the lay priesthood is contained chiefly in two documents, the Constitution on the Church and the Decree on the Apostolate of the Laity. From the first we learn that through Baptism the Christian shares in Christ's priesthood, his prophetic office, and his royal power. He exercises his priesthood by offering up to God all his works, prayers, and apostolic endeavors, his ordinary married and family life, his daily occupations, his physical and mental relaxations, and the hardships of life, and especially by uniting his own self-offering to that of Christ at Mass. He fulfills his prophetic office by giving living witness to the Gospel, especially by a life of faith and charity. Finally, he exercises his share in Christ's kingship by conquering the reign of sin within himself and by leading his brethren to that King for whom to serve is to reign.

The Decree on the Apostolate of the Laity sees the Christian's royal and prophetical priesthood as the foundation of his apostolate, and thus the whole decree becomes a commentary on the lay priesthood. Note the text itself:

The laity share in the priestly, prophetic, and royal office of Christ and therefore *have their own share in the mission of the Church and in the world.* (§ 2; emphasis added)

2. *A Statement of the Doctrine*

Thus far we have pointed to some of the theologians and movements that have influenced the Church's teaching on the lay priesthood. Now we shall have to focus upon the doctrine itself, setting it out as clearly and comprehensively as possible. This we shall do in several steps, some already familiar and needing only to be recalled, others new and requiring explanation.

a. A man is incorporated into Christ's priesthood by being incorporated into his body, the Church. This takes place at Baptism, and we can say without fear of being mistaken that all who are validly baptized have received a permanent share in Christ's priesthood. At the same time we know that Christ can unite men to himself in other ways than the sacrament of Baptism. Thus it becomes impossible to say whether or not this or that non-baptized person belongs to Christ's priestly community. It is quite possible that many persons could belong to it without even realizing it themselves. Regarding who is and who is not united to Christ, the dictum of Augustine is perennially true: "Judge not, unless you wish to be wrong."

b. Within the sacrament of Baptism the rite that symbolizes participation in Christ's priesthood is the post-baptismal anointing. Under the Old Law, men were consecrated as priests and kings by having their heads anointed with sacred oil. Under the New Law, after being washed by the waters of Baptism the individual is anointed with chrism as a way of signifying to him and to others that he now shares Christ's royal and sacerdotal dignity. Of itself this rite does not confer such priesthood; that is accomplished by the actual baptism itself.

c. The sacrament of Baptism has two principal effects, and each of them is, in its own way, a sacerdotal consecration. First, there is the *grace* of Baptism; second, there is the *character* of Baptism. It is worth noting that the non-baptized person who is united to Christ shares in his priesthood only through grace, and not through the character. Not having the character, he does not have the power to unite himself to Christ's sacramental action within the Church. For example, were he to attend Mass he would lack the capacity to unite his self-offering to that of Christ in the Eucharist. On the other hand, having grace, he would have the power to offer nonliturgical spiritual sacrifices, and these sacrifices would be, like Christ's own, redemptive— for himself and for others.

d. The grace conferred by Baptism is *priestly grace*. This calls for explanation. Baptism is a death-dealing, life-giving sacrament. The old man dies, the new man is born. But this mystical death-and-resurrection is not in all respects the same as natural death. For when a man dies naturally, he is completely dead; his body has no life in it. But when a man dies mystically (as in Baptism), he is radically dead, radically cut off from the source of his subjection to evil. Yet the power of evil still lives in him. The grace of Baptism is incessantly at work to complete the death-causing work that it initiates. How does it do this?

It does it by continually impelling us to surrender more and more of ourselves to God until we are totally united to him. It engages us in a lifelong pasch, a lifelong crucifixion and resurrection. It is forever drawing us and nailing us to the cross, to absolute and total acceptance of God's will. Thus this grace involves us in a perpetual movement toward self-donation, toward self-emptying, toward *sacrifice*. And the more one submits to it the stronger it becomes, incorporating us ever more profoundly into the death and resurrection of Christ. Therefore, when we say that baptismal grace is priestly grace, we mean only this: that this grace continually draws us and beckons us toward sacrifice, toward self-surrender.

e. The character conferred by Baptism endows its possessors with priestly power. Once again, let us explain. Christ, our heavenly high priest, continues to serve mankind. And he does this principally (although not solely) through a unique kind of sign-action: the sacraments and sacramentals of the Church.

Now, a man cannot take part in these grace-conferring sign-actions unless Christ has empowered him to participate in his heavenly ministry. The character of Baptism does just that: it enables men to join themselves to Christ in his sacramental worship of the Father. It enables them to take part in this worship and to be sanctified by it.

To appreciate this it is of the utmost importance that we cease to consider the sacraments and sacramentals of the Church as being primarily grace-giving realities. This they are. That is certain. But primarily and fundamentally they are acts of worship, liturgy, prayer. The holiness that we acquire through them results not so much from a spiritual injection from on high as from a personal (yet Christ-assisted and Church-assisted) entrance into a deeper relation with God.

For example, the holiness accruing to us through a fervent reception of the Eucharist results from the Christ-effected faith and devotion that accompanies our reception. There is nothing in any way automatic about our growth in holiness. It is always the effect of our personal faith and our personal worship, assisted and complemented by the worship of Christ and of the Church.

The sacraments and sacramentals of the Church are, then, primarily acts of Christian worship, and the character conferred by Baptism enables us to engage in this worship. It enables us to unite our worship to that of Christ and his Church and thereby to be sanctified. This being so, we believe that St. Thomas chose poorly when he selected the word "passive" to describe the character of Baptism. It suggests that the role of the baptized person in the Church's sacramental life is just that —passive. We prefer the word "incorporative," for this character enables us to incorporate our worship into the worship of Christ.

In three distinct ways the participation in Christ's priesthood that flows from the character of Baptism differs from that which flows from grace. First, grace can be lost, whereas the character cannot be. Second, one's participation in Christ's priesthood through grace can increase (because we can increase in grace), whereas that which comes through the character always remains the same. Third, grace can come to us in countless ways, whereas the character comes only from Baptism. In short, our participation in Christ's priesthood through grace is dynamic and changing, whereas that which comes through the character is static and unchanging.

f. Like Baptism, the sacrament of Confirmation has two principal effects: grace and character. Again as in Baptism, both these effects are sacerdotal consecrations. Thus the question arises: In what respect does Confirmation add to or modify the priesthood imparted by Baptism?

The answer to this question is contained in the description of Confirmation as the sacrament of "Christian maturity." This does not mean that every confirmed person is *de facto* a mature Christian. Rather, it means that such Christians have been given the right and the responsibility and the radical power to assume an *adult* role within the visible Church.

What is this adult role? Both children and adults have responsibilities. But the responsibility proper to youth is a responsibility to receive—to learn, to listen, to be guided, to accept commands, to follow, to respond. The adult, on the other hand, has also a responsibility to give, to help, to contribute, to assist, to lead. He is expected to be a contributing member of the society in which he lives. When, therefore, we say that Confirmation establishes a Christian as an adult within the Church, we mean that henceforth he is committed to take an active part in the Church's mission and that he is responsible for the well-being of the Church.

We also mean—and this is the heart of the matter—that as a

result of his reception of this sacrament his actions in behalf of the Church are united to the action of Christ himself. His actions become sacramental actions—that is, both signs and causes of Christ's action within the world. Thus the sacrament of Confirmation "ordains" the Christian for the apostolate. It empowers him to give efficacious witness to Christ's action in the Church and in the world.

Seen in this light, Baptism and Confirmation together constitute the full initiation into Christian life. Baptism enables one to unite himself to Christ's work of worshiping the Father. Confirmation empowers one to enter into Christ's work of sanctifying the world.

The grace of Baptism creates amity and unity between God and the baptized person so that he can go to him as a son goes to his father. The grace of Confirmation generates a fearless and generous apostolic spirit in those who do not resist it. The character of Baptism enables a man to join in Christ's sacramental worship, and the character of Confirmation empowers him to give sacramental expression to Christ's love for the world.

g. Our final point concerns the relation between the fully constituted lay priest and the ordained or ministerial priest. Let us state at the outset and as emphatically as possible that the lay priesthood *is not* a participation in the priesthood of the minister. We have here two different yet complementary participations in the one priesthood of Christ, and they are related to one another not as greater-and-lesser, but as diverse realities issuing from an infinitely rich unity. To hold the opposite view is extremely dangerous, for it implicitly involves a clericalization of the laity and a distortion of the true nature of the Mystical Body.

At the same time, however, let us not forget that the ordained priest is himself still a lay priest. Upon ordination the priest does not suddenly become unbaptized or unconfirmed. No, he retains those powers, and acquires others not possessed by the layman—powers qualifying him to be a spiritual leader of the lay priesthood. He is chosen *from* the Christian community, and *for* that community. He is called to serve it and, in a sense, to re-create it. Through his preaching and teaching, through his celebration of the liturgy, and through his pastoral guidance, he works for the formation of a community that will vigorously exercise its royal and prophetical priesthood.

Both the layman and the ordained priest are engaged in the same ultimate work. Although the two ministries are essentially distinct, they are nonetheless interrelated. The effective implementation of Christ's work in the world demands their wholehearted cooperation.

We cannot close this section without some consideration of the ministerial priesthood in itself, and this, not only because confusion is widespread in this area, but also because by specifying the role of the ministerial priest we can acquire a clearer idea of the mission of the layman. What, then, is a priest? To what and for what are men ordained?

The usual answer, of course, is that they are mediators, that they stand between God and man, communicating God's light and life to men and offering man's prayers and sacrifices to God. This is not completely unsatisfactory, except that it does not say enough. True, a priest *is* a mediator, especially at Mass and in the confessional, and ideally in the pulpit. But for most priests that accounts for about ten or twelve hours out of the week. What are priests the rest of the time? What are they when they are having dinner with a parishioner, or watching teen-agers rehearse a play, or attending a CFM meeting? Mediators? Maybe.

Another answer is that the priest is primarily the catalyst or, let us even say, the creator of the Christian community. His role, whether he is stationed in a prison, or a hospital, or a school, or a parish, is to form a Christian community, to awaken a sense of community, to inspire the characteristic activities of such a community. This conception appeals to me more than that of mediator for the reason that today the idea of mediator suggests distance and separation rather than unity and identification with those he is serving. A mediator in a wage dispute, for example, is chosen from among those who belong neither to union nor to management.

And yet, to define the priesthood in terms of forming a Christian community is not without its own dangers and limitations. After all, every Christian is called to do this. Every Christian is responsible for the formation of this community. So we are left with our original question: What is the specific contribution of the priest?

One instructive way in which to confront this problem is to ask whether a priest should be described primarily in terms of his ministry of the word, or in terms of his sacramental ministry, particularly the Mass. Now, there can be no doubt that just as Christ's death was the central and consummating act of his own priestly ministry, so the sacramental re-enactment of that death is the central and consummating act of the ministerial priesthood. Few would question this, although none of us can ever appreciate it enough. And yet, how much of the average priest's time is spent celebrating Mass and administering the other sacraments? A quarter? A fifth? Probably not more than that.

Moreover, with some obvious exceptions the administration of the sacraments is not overly difficult. A substantial part of it is mechanical and does not constitute a serious challenge. And it is precisely this—this lack of challenge in the priesthood understood as primarily a sacramental ministry—that causes many young priests to question the value of their calling and to drift deeper and deeper into social work, psychology, or secular scholarship. But in doing this they may be making a mistake. For just as men have a right to good medicine from a doctor, and good legal counsel from a lawyer, so they have a right to a specific service from their priests and ministers. What is this specific service?

I would call it "spiritual direction." I would say that a priest can adequately define his social role in terms of *a ministry of the word,* and, if I may be pardoned a reference to one of the mottos of my Order, I would suggest that "contemplata aliis tradere"—to contemplate and to communicate to others—might serve as a grounding principle for the whole priestly ministry.

To contemplate—both the Word of God and the word of man, both the city of God and the city of man—in order to unite the two, in order continually to renew the mystery of the Word made flesh. To contemplate, not only books and ideas, but more especially people, the people we are called to live with and work for. And this means getting to know and love them; it means entering their lives, and letting them into ours. And then to communicate—to make one's own life a communication of divine life, and specifically to approach one's contemporaries with the same message that Christ addressed to his. And, may I add, to communicate not only by proclaiming the Word oneself but also by inspiring and initiating dialogue, mutual exploration of the mysteries of life.

* * *

The next three chapters will explore some of the ways in which the layman can realize the apostolic potential in the priesthood of Christians that we have just propounded. The first chapter will cover the layman's prophetic ministry as it informs the lay apostolate; the second, his pastoral ministry; and lastly, his priestly ministry.

To his contemporaries Jesus Christ was a rabbi or teacher, not a priest or a king. He was, however, not an ordinary teacher, for "unlike the Scribes, he taught them with authority" (Mark 1:22). And his message was backed by miracles ("signs," as St. John called them) that lent credibility to his teaching. For these reasons many people regarded him as a prophet.

The man born blind, when asked by the Pharisees who had opened his eyes, answered, "He is a prophet" (John 9:17). In the week preceding his death, when strangers in Jerusalem were asking about the man who was causing all the commotion, the townspeople answered, "This is the prophet Jesus from Nazareth of Galilee" (Matt. 21:11). Then, when Christ himself asked the Apostles what men thought of him, they answered in terms of prophetic figures. Some, they said, believed he was John the Baptist risen again, and others thought he was Elijah returned from heaven, and still others looked upon him as a new prophet sent from God.

What is a prophet? Is he a person who sees into the future and tells of events to come? Not necessarily. This may or may not be part of his mission. A man might not have the slightest intimation of future occurrences and still be a prophet. For a prophet is simply a man called by God to proclaim a specific and distinctive message to the men with whom he lives. His task, as Professor Lindblom has pointed out, is not so much

95

to *foretell* as it is to *forthtell*.[26] He is a person who feels compelled to communicate, compelled to say what he has seen and
heard, and compelled to go where he has been commanded to
go. Moreover, he is a person whose activity issues from passivity
and whose radical freedom and independence issue from absolute subjection to and dependence upon God.

A prophet is a sign and a giver of signs. He cannot help but
create tension between himself and other human beings. For
he witnesses to something that he insists cannot be disregarded.
He witnesses to something that calls for either acceptance or
rejection. The more perfect the prophet the more does he become a sign of contradiction. Compared to Christ, every other
prophet is a minor prophet. His words went deeper. His message was more absolute. His claims were more "preposterous."
More, much more, was at stake in accepting or rejecting him.
Upon that division the final destiny of every man is determined.

A Christian is called to be a prophet in The Prophet, a sign
of The Sign, a sacrament of The Sacrament—Jesus Christ. His
mission is like that of John the Baptist. He is "to prepare the
way," to prepare the soil of humanity for the seed of grace.
Where, when, and how that seed will be planted, he cannot be
sure. He seeks only to warm and open the human soul in order
that when Christ does come to it he might bear much fruit.

The Christian fulfills his prophetic ministry (as Christ did
his) by giving signs of God's love and present concern for men.
In a sense these signs are "miracles," and like Christ's own
miracles they are victories of the power of life over the power
of death, and of the power of love over the power of hate. These
"everyday miracles" are images of the miracle of all miracles—
Christ's resurrection. They infuse life into a world that has
been condemned to death. They witness to Christ's victory over
sin and death, and as such, they hold out hope, hope that beyond death there lies new life.

To be a prophet after the manner of Christ involves seeing

oneself as Christ saw himself—as a man "sent" by God, as a man entrusted with a message. This way of seeing oneself is not acquired easily. It comes only to those whose lives are centered in Christ and surrendered to him. For only thus can men experience to the full the transforming power of the Word of God, and only thus will there develop within them an ever more active desire to communicate it. In short, *a Christian is an apostle only to the extent that he is a disciple.*

A. FORMS OF CHRISTIAN WITNESS

Here we shall list some of the principal ways in which a Christian can give effective witness to his faith.

The liturgy. Through participation in the liturgy, and particularly through participation in the Mass, the Christian community reminds itself of its own identity and professes that identity to the world. Ideally, through liturgical expression of their faith, Christians should acquire an ever deeper realization and an ever deeper appreciation of what they are and what they are called to be. Ideally, the liturgical expression of the faith should engender its extraliturgical expression. Ideally, the liturgy should move us into the apostolate, and the apostolic action should call us back to the liturgy. Each needs the other, and a full Christian life needs them both.

The witness of presence. Insignificant as it may seem, simply being *present* to other people (humanly and personally present) is the indispensable requirement of all witness, and sometimes—quite often, in fact—it is about all that we can do. For example, all that Mary could do on Calvary was *be there.* Yet that in itself was a sign to Jesus and to all around of the depth of her love and loyalty.

To be humanly present to another means more than mere physical presence. It means intellectual, emotional, and spiritual presence as well. It means laying aside everything in order to give ourselves completely to those with whom we are. To be truly present to another person is to be wholly receptive to him, wholly attentive to him. It is a creative kind of presence, for it invites the other to be and to express his whole self.

The witness of communal existence. To live in communion with others involves a willingness to share: to let others know what we think and feel, to let them know who we are. It involves leaving the door of one's heart and soul ajar, so that others may come in and stay if they'd like. More difficult yet, it means being willing to go outside the hearth of our own lives into the lives of whoever might ask us in. In short, it means developing a capacity to share what we have and are, a capacity to give and receive—deeply, humanly, personally.

This is no easy task. It is the work of a lifetime, a work that grows as we grow, a work that is born of the realization that one has much to give and much to receive. Difficult though it is, there is no deeper or more telling expression of what it means to live in Christ than that of a person who is open and free and accessible to his fellow men.

Non-verbal witness. "What you *are* speaks so loudly, we cannot hear what you *say.*" There are dozens, and perhaps hundreds, of ways in which we communicate without ever saying a word.

To mention but a few: the look in one's eyes, the expression on one's face, the tone of the voice, the way one sits or stands or gestures, the attention with which one listens, the ease or lack thereof with which one relates to others, the way one reacts to the fortunate and unfortunate occurrences of life, the way one laughs, the things one owns, the clothes one wears, the books one reads, the entertainments one enjoys, the whole mode and manner of life. All these things say something, and today they say more than ever before, because men have learned not to trust words alone.

This form of communication provides Christians with count-less opportunities for effective witness. The small thoughtful-ness, the welcome that one gives to another, the sensitivity with which one responds to others (rejoicing with those who rejoice and weeping with those who weep), the visit, the gift, the post-card, the telephone call, the spirit with which one works and plays with others—Christ is active in all of these things, express-ing himself through ourselves, communicating his love through our love.

The witness of the word. Without minimizing the value and importance of non-verbal or silent witness, we wish to state plainly that this by itself is not sufficient. The Decree on the Apostolate of the Laity states this twice:

[The lay apostolate] . . . does not consist only in the witness of one's way of life; a true apostle looks for opportunities to announce Christ by words. (§ 6)

And later, referring to the formation that should be given to Christians in view of their apostolic responsibilities, the docu-ment reads:

In regard to the apostolate for evangelizing and sanctifying men, the laity must be specially formed to engage in conversa-tion *with others, believers or non-believers, in order to mani-fest Christ's message to all men.* (§ 31; emphasis added)

The Church provides a wide variety of services. It feeds the hungry, clothes the naked, shelters the poor; it cares for the sick, instructs the young and the old, and prays for the living and the dead. But in the mind of Christ all these services are subordinate to the service of communicating the Gospel. It is not bread, or medicine, or clothing, or money, or shelter, or even learning that saves, but living faith in the Word of God.

Yet few seem willing to provide this service of all services. Nine Christians out of ten are more hesitant to get involved in the ministry of the Word than any other apostolic work.

There are several reasons for this. Many Christians do not regard themselves as sufficiently grounded in the faith to communicate it to others in a verbal way. Many others, conscious of their spiritual failings, do not feel justified in evangelizing others. Moreover, in our country there has been a tradition that religion is something that is not to be openly discussed except with one's closest friends, and then rarely. Finally, and perhaps most importantly, there is fear—fear of being misunderstood, fear of the way in which others will react, fear of taking a stand, fear of rejection by one's friends and associates.

In order to overcome these obstacles, three steps can be taken. First, the layman must be *called*. Although Baptism and Confirmation in themselves constitute such a call, there is no substitute for a personal invitation to undertake some specific work of communicating Christian truth. In the Parable of the Laborers in the Vineyard the householder goes out to the marketplace at the eleventh hour and asks: "Why do you stand here all day idle?" To which the "idlers" responded: *"Because no man has hired us"* (Matt. 20:7).

Second, men must be *trained* for this ministry, for it requires skill as well as motivation. This implies advanced instruction both in the faith itself and in the art of communicating it in a manner that is interesting and attractive, sincere and yet not solemn, personal rather than "bookish," and, above all, relevant to life.

Third, the fear of initiating dialogue on religious matters must be overcome. The ideal way to overcome such inhibitions is to begin discussing such subjects with one's closest, most trusted friends, and there to learn how to speak about them without seeming officious or "pious," and without trying to force one's own convictions upon others. This is the way in which Christ brought along his Apostles. It is also the way in which parents can form one another and their children.

Finally, we should recognize that although both the layman and the ordained priest have a ministry of the Word, they are not called to exercise this ministry in precisely the same way. The layman *witnesses* to and *professes* his faith. But neither his witness nor his profession is authoritative. He speaks as one Christian to another or as a Christian to a non-Christian. His style or approach is "unofficial." It will be an expression of his personal faith, and as such, he will be heard not so much because of *what* he is as because of *who* he is.

Professional witness. The artist, the novelist, the poet, the musician, the playwright, the journalist, the lay theologian— such men are professionally involved in the arts of communication. Never before has their work been so important to the Church and to the world as it is today, for never before has their influence been so great.

Their apostolate consists in uniting artistic or professional excellence to their view of life and thus to give profound expression to the faith that is in them. They are not asked to be propagandists. Nor are they expected to whitewash Christianity. No, what is asked of them is asked of every Christian: to deepen their faith and then to express it in their life and work. In this, Dante is perhaps the supreme exemplar. By bringing beauty to the service of truth, artists exercise an almost indispensable function in the Church.

Contemporary witness. Every age puts a premium on certain human qualities, and people who embody these qualities have every chance of making great impact upon their contemporaries. Among the qualities that are singularly impressive to the men of our time the first is *joy*. In today's world deep and abiding joy is a kind of miracle, and when men see it they are struck with wonder and admiration. They are attracted to it; they want to remain in its presence.

Second, there is *warmth*. In a world that moves too fast to foster affection and is characterized by fear and mistrust, those who emanate genuine personal friendliness and affection can communicate at a deeper and more profound level than others. People are instinctively more open with them and more at ease.

Then there is *honesty*. By this more is meant than merely telling the truth; it means *being* true, and what is more, being *expressively* true—not hiding what one is, nor disguising it, but revealing it without exaggeration or pretension. This requires courage and self-detachment; it inspires trust and candor. Those who have these qualities have been given a tremendous opportunity to serve Christ in a particularly effective way.

Group witness. All that has been said thus far about personal witness might have been said with equal validity of community or group witness. On the other hand, things may be said of community witness that cannot be said of personal witness. For whereas individual witness sacramentalizes Christ, collective witness also sacramentalizes the community that he founded. Take, for example, the witness that a family, the basic unit of the community, can give.

Every family has its own spirit, and this spirit reveals itself in many ways: in thoughtfulness and affection, in cooperation and helpfulness, in understanding and appreciation, in the way they disagree and in the way they agree. There is no need to say what the ideal Christian family should be. But there is need to say that such families should witness to what they are, and that one of the best ways to do this is through *hospitality*.

The Christian home should be like the Church itself—an open community wherein all are welcome, a place where hearts may be renewed and refreshed. It should be a compassionate community, quick in the service of its own members and of its neighbors. Furthermore, husbands and wives, through their mutual fidelity and deep solicitude for one another, do yeoman service for their neighbors and especially for their children, simply by giving living testimony to the fact that marriage *can work*.

B. RULES FOR EFFECTIVE WITNESS

We have been considering various ways in which Christian witness can be given. No doubt there are many others. Let us now think about the qualities that make that witness Christlike and efficacious.

First, and perhaps most importantly, our ability to move others depends upon our capacity to be moved by them. Or, in other words, our ability to give signs depends upon our capacity to receive them. Otherwise our message will not be relevant. It will not be attuned to the mode in which others are thinking and speaking.

This calls for sensitivity. It supposes a talent for "getting the feel" of those with whom we live and speak. Experienced counselors and trained salesmen are usually excellent at this. Quickly they sense what approach will or will not work with a particular individual. Almost intuitively they realize what will offend and what will appeal. Similarly, professional speakers acquire an instinct for what will strike the minds and move the hearts of their audiences. For those of us who lack these skills, there is still hope. For the more we love and understand people, the more sensitive will we be in communicating with them. Above all, we must *listen*, humbly, perseveringly, willingly.

The second requirement is similar to the first. Men are moved most deeply by those with whom they can *identify*. This was one of the secrets of Christ's appeal and, more recently, of the appeal of Pope John. In every way Christ "belonged" to his people. He shared their poverty, their labors, their subjection. He spoke their language. He sang their songs. He loved their festivals. Because he was "one of them," men could feel that he understood them.

And so must it be for today's Christian who wishes to have apostolic impact upon his brothers. If he looks down upon them, if in any way he patronizes them, if he cannot enjoy what they enjoy and appreciate what they appreciate, if he is quick to reject and slow to accept the things that make up their lives, those whom he has been sent to help will pass him by unaffected and unmoved, no matter how good or holy he may be.

The third characteristic of effective Christian witness is *genuineness*. It cannot be "phony." The least falsification of self atrophies one's whole apostolic endeavor, and lends credibility to the contention that our faith is not for real people.

Phoniness is not always deliberate. More often than not, it is a result of immaturity. Either not knowing or not accepting his real self, the phony plays a role. He is inflated, false, self-important, and therefore a danger to the apostolate. For every one person whom he attracts to Christ he will repel five, and what is perhaps worse, he discredits apostolic activity in the minds of young people.

The fourth characteristic of effective witness is *directness*. This means saying what one means, and meaning what one says. It means squaring with people, leveling with them, and not working solely by innuendo or allusion. There should be no ambiguity about our witness. It should be as clear and straightforward as possible. Christ said: "Let your light *shine* before men, in order that they may see your good works and give glory to your Father in heaven" (Matt. 5:16). In practice, this means that we should not only *be* concerned about others but that we should give manifest expression to that concern. They may not want it, they may not need it, but then again they may; and if we have hidden it, they will have no way of reaching for it.

Finally, our witness should be characterized by *fidelity*. It cannot be Yes today and No tomorrow. People will not trust a prophet who contradicts himself or whose words speak louder than his actions. True witness is a day-in day-out affair. Christ's own witness was singularly consistent. Everything that he said and did was of a piece, and hence men had no doubts where he stood or about the sincerity of his convictions.

How does this apply to today's apostle? For one thing, it commits him to a lifelong struggle to uproot those aspects of his character which do not reflect Christ—like impatience, envy, pettiness, and self-pity. For another, it means that, come what may, he will honor his apostolic commitments and perform them with care and thoroughness.

C. DEFINING ONE'S APOSTOLATE

Suppose that a Christian, conscious of his prophetic ministry, works at becoming ever more passive to the action of the Holy Spirit within him; suppose also that he is aware of the many ways in which he can give witness and of the qualities that will make that witness effective. There still remains one important thing for him to do. He must define his apostolate. He must discover precisely where his apostolic responsibilities lie.

Here, of course, there is no room for rigidity. Remembering always the Parable of the Good Samaritan, he will respond to human needs wherever he encounters them. Nevertheless, like Christ himself, he will circumscribe his apostolic activity. For if he spreads himself too thin or if he confuses his primary and secondary responsibilities, he will do little or nothing of real value.

Actually it is not difficult to discover the people toward whom we have a primary apostolic responsibility. These are the members of our own family and our close friends. Inevitably we exert a deep and lasting influence upon these people (and they on us), either for good or for bad. By the way we relate to them, by our attitude toward them, by our interest and concern for them, and by our own personal integrity, we can continually foster their natural and supernatural development.

In this primary area of our apostolate, mere omission can be destructive. Indifference, not to mention positive hostility, can be disastrous. The husband or wife who simply does not care about his or her spouse, the parent who lets his children drift, the "friend" who watches his neighbor sink—these people often do more damage than open enemies. Family, friends, fellow workers: these are the ones for whom God has made us most responsible. Such is the circle in which God has situated us and to which he has called us.

For those Catholics who have the time and generosity to devote themselves to some additional apostolate, two factors are important. First, they should consider the *needs* of those around them: the needs of the parish, the neighborhood, the city. Once a particular need has been focused upon, they can either enter a group already at work on it or form a group of their own for the specific purpose of meeting a particular need.

Secondly, they should take stock of their own abilities. For example, the man who has little understanding or appreciation of sports could choose more wisely than to offer his services to the community recreation center. And the person who is completely unfamiliar with politics will hardly do his best work in the neighborhood political organization. The lay apostle is not called to undertake any and every activity, but to make apostolic use of the interests and talents that he has. Thus, the lawyer and doctor are being superbly apostolic in serving clients and patients who cannot afford to pay. And the skilled laborer is doing the same when he puts his skills to work for some needy neighbor.

We should like to close this section by presenting what we consider to be the principal pastoral problem connected with Christian witness. The Christian is called to be a sign, and as

such he should signify something beyond himself—namely
Christ. The difficulty is this: How can a Christian make it evident (for a good sign is evident) that his good works and charitable actions originate in Christ? Will those who see him see
Christ in him? Will those who are drawn to him thereby be
drawn to Christ? In other words, in what way does the witness
actually communicate Christ?

He is, we say, a "sacramental person"—that is, he communicates Christ through his sign-activity. But he is not sacramental
in the same way as are the seven sacraments. He does not *cause*
an infusion of sanctifying grace into the soul; rather, he is an
occasion of such grace. He opens hearts and readies them for
Christ's visitation. His very life constitutes a call and an inspiration to be converted, to change, to become better. In this,
his task is like that of John the Baptist. It is the task of leveling
the road and making straight the path for Christ.

Two different words—"royal" and "pastoral"—are used to describe this aspect of the lay apostolate. Neither of them is completely satisfactory. To those accustomed to democratic institutions, the first ("royal") bespeaks the despotism of absolute monarchs and evokes images of wealth and pomp and autocratic living. Yet the word is part of our oldest traditions and cannot be lightly dismissed. The fact is that Christ is our King and Lord and that we share in his kingship. Let it then stand, but let us not misunderstand its meaning.

Our kingship, like Christ's own, is a form of service. "Among pagans it is the kings who lord it over them. . . . This must not happen with you. No; the greatest among you must behave as if he were the youngest, the leader as if he were the one who serves" (Luke 22:25–26). Our kingship consists in serving men by serving Christ, and in serving Christ by serving men. "In so far as you did this to one of the least of these brothers of mine, you did it to me" (Matt. 25:40).

The second word—"pastoral"—has had a more fortunate history, and is not weighed down with the unfortunate connotations of the first. It is Scriptural. Christ regarded himself as a pastor, a shepherd. "I am the good shepherd; I know my own, and my own know me" (John 10:14). Christians share in Christ's pastorate. They are pastors in The Pastor, shepherds in The Shepherd. There is really only one reason why we hesitate to describe this particular aspect of the Christian ministry as "pastoral," and this is that the word usually refers to the totality of apostolic work rather than to any specific part of it.

In distinguishing the layman's prophetic and royal functions we do not wish to imply that some apostolic works are purely prophetic while others are strictly royal. No, these are but two different dimensions of all apostolic activity. All such works are both royal and prophetic—that is, all of them contain both power (and are therefore royal) and meaning (and hence are prophetic). Take, for example, a civil rights demonstration. As prophetic, it calls attention to a particular social injustice; as royal, it is a vehicle of power and influence. Actions are prophetic inasmuch as they convey *meaning;* they are royal inasmuch as they exercise *influence.*

In his book *The Power to Love,* Dr. Martin Luther King indicates how closely these two functions are related. He says that thousands of people are losing confidence in nonviolent solutions to the social impasses in which they find themselves, and that these people urgently need *signs* of the sincerity of society's concern for them. Unless signs are forthcoming, they will in all likelihood turn to violence. On the other hand, if such signs are kept before their eyes they will take hope and will regain the *power* to love. Thus, the signs themselves possess power. The two ministries are inextricably bound together.

The layman's royal ministry involves two complementary activities: one negative and one positive. Negatively, there is the work of winter, of death, of exorcism; of diminishing and removing evil in all its forms. Positively, there is the work of spring and resurrection; the work of renewing hearts and minds and bodies.

These two activities go hand-in-hand. Neither can succeed without the other. Where the first (the work of reform) exists without the second (the work of renewal), the evil will be removed without replacing it by good, and the devil will return, bringing with him "seven other spirits more evil than itself, . . . so that the man ends up by being worse than he was before" (Matt. 12:45). On the other hand, neither can renewal take place without reform, and for the same reason that health cannot be restored until disease is destroyed.

Several years ago certain French thinkers proposed the theory that the work of divinization (the whole positive aspect of our ministry) should not be begun until the negative work (the elimination of large-scale social evils) was well on its way to completion. As Montuclard put it,

We do not think religion can be made to blossom from rottenness, so for the present we have no other aim than to work in cooperation with all men of good will for the prevention of war, and toward the coming of a society built on foundations more reasonable and more human. Then, and only then, will it be possible to attack rightly the religious problem.[27]

While these theologians contributed greatly toward making Christians aware of their societal responsibilities, their theory by-passed the fact that the work of divinization is itself humanizing and that ultimately nothing so profoundly humanizes men and situation as do faith and charity. Therefore it would be a mistake to separate one's apostolic labors into two phases: one for humanization and another for divinization. Both should be pursued from beginning to end.

In exercising his pastoral ministry the Christian will be mindful of his limitations. He will realize that only God can get to the roots of human evil. As the Pharisees themselves said, "Only God can forgive sins." Similarly, no man, by and of himself, can make other men more holy. This, too, is a work of God. Our role is always dispositive. And yet, as one playwright put it, "God needs men."

Strange as it may sound, through our apostolic action we give

God the opportunity to exercise his far more salient action. In the work of redeeming the world, God and men are collaborators. Each in his own way contributes to the total effectiveness of the action. Thus, if it is true to say that in this work man cannot do without God, it is equally true that God cannot do without men. Paul spoke of this when he said: "How are they to believe him whom they have not heard? And how are they to hear, if no one preaches?" (Rom. 10:14). Men depend upon God, surely; but so also God is depending upon men.

A. FORMS OF CHRISTIAN EXORCISM

Usually when we think of exorcism we think of Christ or of certain men specially approved to help "possessed souls." Or we recall the two men who roamed the graveyard at Gerasa and how a legion of devils were struck from them into a herd of swine. We think of striking instances of Christ's power over evil, and we forget that we share in that power. All of us are engaged in Christ's conquest of Satan; all of us are called to be "exorcists." Let us therefore explore some of the ways in which we can actuate this ministry.

Exorcising oneself. "What a wretched man I am!" said Paul. "Instead of doing the good things I want to do, I carry out the sinful things I do not want" (Rom. 7:24, 19).

Throughout his life, Paul was anguished by an internal alien force bent on destroying him. He fought that force with all the vehemence of his being, yet he could never completely subdue it. Nor can we. But with God's help we can extricate more and more of ourselves from its grasp. Vicious habits can be broken one by one, passions can be tamed, selfishness can be countered, hostility can be neutralized. How? By obeying the Word, by enforcing the inspirations that the Holy Spirit sends us, by surrendering ourselves to the action of Christ in the sacraments, and by incorporating his spirit into our daily lives.

We exorcise ourselves through *prayer,* and *sacrifice,* and *mortification.* We exorcise ourselves when we *examine our consciences,* thereby focusing and directing our moral energy to one or two specific failings. We exorcise ourselves through the patient endurance of *suffering,* accepting it as the action of the Divine Physician cleansing our souls more profoundly than we could ever have done by ourselves. We exorcise ourselves through *fidelity* to daily duties, and through exposing ourselves to Christ's influence: to men through whom he acts, to books through which he speaks, to silence in which he draws us to himself. And finally, we can exorcise ourselves through *action,* charitable action, apostolic action.

Exorcising one's neighbor. There are many ways in which we can deliver our neighbor from evil: by prayer, by sacrifice, by leading him away from occasions of sin, by good example, by inspiration, by helping him up when he falls, by encouragement, by respect, by concern. One of the most direct ways is *fraternal guidance.* St. Augustine once said: "If your neighbor has a sickness of the body of which he is unaware, would it not be cruel of you to conceal it from him? Yet, how much more cruel it is if you do not correct the sins of his heart" (Rule of St. Augustine).

When we truly love someone we accept him as he is, but at the same time we will not allow him to destroy himself—physically, emotionally, or spiritually. Be it something so simple as encouraging a tired friend to get some rest, or something so grave as commiting him to an institution where he can get proper care, charity impels the Christian to action when he sees his neighbor sinking.

To guide, to counsel, to correct: these are not tasks to be taken lightly. They call for humility, for honesty, and above all, for deep respect and love of those toward whom we exercise this ministry. It calls for courage, too: the courage to be direct and honest, a courage similar to that of a doctor who occasionally must hurt people in order to help them. Finally, it calls for tact, for a sense of the proper time and place, and for a mode of communicating that is clear and direct, and yet respectful and careful.

Less obviously but even more importantly, men keep one another spiritually and psychologically strong through the every-day respect and appreciation that they manifest toward one another. For the man who is appreciated will appreciate himself, and the man who is respected will respect himself; and both self-appreciation and self-respect are vitally important for full Christian living. The same can be said of love. Only those who have received it can fully develop their capacity to give it. Therefore, simply in admiring and loving someone we are enhancing his Christian and apostolic potential.

Exorcising our environment. Human life is profoundly influenced by the environment in which it is lived. The relative beauty or ugliness of one's neighborhood, its available recreational facilities, the clubs and local organizations to which one belongs, the "character" and spirit of the neighborhood, the amount of money one earns, the kind of dwelling in which one lives, the education one has received—most of these things are taken for granted yet all of them mold us, for better or for worse.

Whenever social forces constrict human development, whenever they force human beings to live inhumanly, there is reason for exorcism—*communal* exorcism. Communal, because in our day the individual by himself is no match for social evils. Poverty, delinquency, drug addiction, and syndicated injustice are so deeply embedded in the social fabric of some cultures that only the united efforts of many persons can hope to uproot them. And the day is fast passing when each religion could hope to cope with these problems by setting up its own social agencies. The time has come for ecumenical action in all of these areas.

This does not mean that long-established Catholic, Protestant, and Jewish organizations should amalgamate themselves into ecumenical bodies. But it does mean that they should at least coordinate their efforts and assist each other in every way possible. And it also means that Catholics should feel free and, in fact, should be encouraged to cooperate with their Protestant and Jewish neighbors in community development. Apostolic action need not bear an apostolic label. One can often do as much for Christ in a nondenominational interracial council as in "Catholic" council devoted to the same objectives.

The need for communal action should not blind us to the dangers that invariably accompany institutionalized apostolates: the danger of becoming remote from the very problems that they wish to solve; the danger of spending too much time in talk and not enough in direct action; the danger of becoming more occupied with internal organization than with external action; the danger of not being able to react swiftly to changes in the social situation. There is no way to escape these dangers completely, but if they are recognized and combatted they need not neutralize a community's effectiveness.

As to the manner in which this social ministry should be exercised, Christ is the only perfect exemplar. Note how he responded to *particular needs,* when and where he encountered them. Note how he responded personally and totally. Note how he chose to live among those he wished to help, thus becoming not only his brother's keeper but his brother's brother as well. Note how he broke bread with friend and stranger alike.

The Christlike social worker will be characterized by an ability to *identify* with those among whom he works. Insofar as it is possible, he will share their mentality, their aspirations, their work, their play, their joys and sorrows. He will do these things not so that he might win them to himself but rather so that he might better express the love and truth of Christ among them.

In actual practice, social action must be governed by the

prudence that tells one what is here and now possible. Social action is essentially pragmatic. Ideals are upheld, to be sure, but realities are sought. A park must be cleared; a street must be lighted; a criminal must be prosecuted. Unless a group is willing to descend to particular objectives its social impact will be a matter of words.

Exorcising the international community. It is no longer sufficient to confine one's apostolic perspective to one's own nation or culture. The possibility of nuclear war, the vast and growing imbalance between the rich and the poor nations, the horrendous amounts of capital sunk into armaments and propaganda, the population explosion, the knowledge explosion— these and other factors highlight the necessity of international cooperation. The obligation to foster such cooperation falls, first of all, upon those who govern their national communities, and especially upon those who govern the rich and powerful nations of the earth. For "he who has the greater power also has the greater responsibility."

But what can the individual Christian do? To list but a few of the many ways in which he can contribute to international understanding and development, he can: 1) pray for peace and prosperity; 2) become responsibly aware of the reality that is the modern world; 3) make his convictions known to those responsible for international policies; 4) learn a foreign language; 5) welcome foreign travelers and immigrants; 6) house a foreign student; 7) support the United Nations and its many subsidiary organizations; 8) join the Peace Corps or the Foreign Service; 9) enter a missionary apostolate; 10) contribute to disaster relief.

The exorcising function of work. Work has its effect both on the worker himself and on the society in which he labors. Take, for example, a task as seemingly inconsequential as that of a garbage collector. Without such men, cities would be overwhelmed with filth and disease. Their labors keep city life relatively healthful, orderly, and clean. Furthermore, by being faithful to their work, they strengthen and ennoble their own personalities and provide their families with the means to live dignified human life. Finally, they also exert a significant influence upon one another. Thus, through their work, they can "exorcise" the physical environment, themselves, and their fellow workers.

Some jobs are more influential than others and for that reason, objectively speaking, they offer the Christian greater opportunities to exorcise community life through his work. For example, a politician exerts more influence than a dress designer; a teacher, more than a miner; and a journalist, more than a manufacturer of cake-mix. Nevertheless, it remains true that, subjectively speaking, the important factor is not so much what one does as how one does it.

The worker whose work is an expression of charity constantly betters himself and others through it. On the other hand, if work is done with indifference and slovenliness and if fellow workers are treated in an unfriendly and uncooperative way, the worker degrades both himself and his environment.

The exorcising function of leisure. Of John F. Kennedy it has been said that he knew how to work and he knew how to play. He knew how to make creative use of his free time, and this not only enabled him to work harder and better, but it also helped him to make life more pleasant for all who knew him.

Christians have sometimes placed such a premium on the value of work and suffering that the furtherance of human happiness is made to appear as an almost pagan pursuit, as if Christianity and pleasure were somehow opposed. But this was not Christ's message. Neither joy nor pleasure is sinful. In fact we are never less likely to sin than when we are enjoying ourselves in a wholesome way. The existence of joy in our own lives and in those of our associates removes both us and them from the boredom, ennui, and dissatisfaction that make sin look so desirable.

Thus we see how vastly important is the apostolate of those who provide recreation centers for youth and of those who instruct others in sports, hobbies, and crafts. How essential it is that parents engender in their children correct attitudes toward having fun, and what a benefit they confer upon them by interesting them in some art or sport.

Physically, psychologically, and spiritually, there is no substitute for play, and the child who has not learned how to enjoy himself will enter adulthood seriously handicapped. In having a party, in teaching someone how to ski or swim or play the piano, in being able to help others relax and enjoy themselves, the Christian does a major service for his fellow man. He is acting in unison with God, who created men in order that they might be happy forever.

Exorcising Church practices. Strictly speaking, the layman has no executive, legislative, or judicial authority within the Church. He cannot make laws nor does he have the right to adjudicate in matters of faith and morals. By divine institution, these powers belong only to the pope and the bishops. But this does not mean that the layman is completely devoid of all power in the Christian commonwealth of which he is a member, for power is an analogous reality.

Power actually consists also in all the unofficial measures that lead to and flow from such decisions. It consists in advising and enlightening Church leaders and in constructively criticizing Church practices and institutions. It consists in solid and unswerving witness to what one believes. It consists in presenting new ideas and in discovering new ways to carry on the apostolate. In the Church, changes do not always begin from above. As often as not they begin with the insights and initiatives of individual Christians. This is true in parishes, in dioceses, and in the Church universal.

Pope Pius XII spoke of the need for "public opinion" within the Church, and as a result of the *aggiornamento* this is becoming a reality. Laymen are becoming more and more articulate in expressing their convictions about what the Church should do and be. And this, far from being a sign of disloyalty or weakness of faith, indicates that the Christian community is becoming more vital and alive than it has been for a long time.

B. PORTRAIT OF AN APOSTLE

Inasmuch as the quality of our Christian service depends in no small measure upon our sensitivity to the needs of those whom we are called to serve, the apostolic person should be, first of all, a man of *empathy*. How does he acquire this quality? Principally through love and suffering. Through love, because love makes one attentive to the feelings, needs, and desires of others. Through suffering, because suffering enlarges one's capacity for compassion and deepens one's desire to bring joy into the lives of others.

Louis Veuillot once wrote, "Fortunately for the poor, there are the poor." Those who know what it is to be poor are usually the most responsive to the needs of the poor. The same can be said of other areas in life. "Fortunately for the sinner, there are men with a living awareness of their own capacity for sin. Fortunately for the doubtful and perplexed, there are men who have experienced doubt and perplexity. Fortunately for alcoholics, there are men who have fought the same fight." Empathy, sensitivity, is born of love and tears.

The second human quality that makes for an effective apostolate is *approachability*. When it comes to communicating the deep and personal things of life, men want to be with someone with whom they can feel at ease; someone who they know has their best interest at heart; someone whose life bespeaks understanding and brotherliness. Not someone rigid or cold; not someone distant or aloof; not someone ambitious or domineering.

There are many ways to be unapproachable. One man will manage it by always being "busy," so that others will realize that he has more important things to do than "waste" time with them. Another will be willing to do things *for* people but unwilling to share things *with* them. St. Augustine sensed the difference between the two when he said to the people of Hippo: "What I am for you terrifies me; what I am with you consoles me. For you, I am a bishop; but with you, I am a Christian." [28] Perhaps the easiest and most effective way to achieve a high degree of unapproachability is to be inaccessible, physically and personally: physically, by creating physical barriers between oneself and others (rigid office hours, doors closed, inflexible schedules); personally, by creating personal barriers (fear, hostility, anger, insensitivity).

It is no secret that the most approachable people are those who most readily approach others. Those who instinctively go out to others naturally evoke a similar response in them. This is one of the reasons that Pope John was so popular: he went to others rather than having them come to him. Here again what St. Augustine said is perennially true: "It is always easier for men to return love than it is for them to initiate it."

The apostle should be empathetic. He should be approachable. He should also be a person of *quality*. Quality attracts, whether it be in automobiles, wrist watches, or human beings. By personal quality we mean those aspects of the human personality that are almost universally admired: sincerity, courage, generosity, openness, affability, courtesy, thoughtfulness, and dedication. The apostolic person who lacks these virtues will repel people rather than attract them. He will hinder rather than help the communication of Christ's word.

Finally, he must be *relevant*—relevant in word and relevant in deed. Today men's thoughts revolve around war and peace, around person and community, around freedom and law, around right and wrong, around love and hate, around the meaning of life and death—and about all these things the Gospel has much to say.

The Gospel itself *is* relevant, if only we can communicate it in a way that will touch the hearts of our contemporaries. Deeds, too, must be relevant, and none are more relevant than the corporal and spiritual works of mercy, all of them directed to specific human needs. Might not lay apostles occasionally examine themselves on these fourteen acts of Christian charity? When have I last fed the hungry, given drink to the thirsty, or clothed the naked? How long has it been since I visited the sick, comforted someone in sorrow, counseled someone in doubt? Have I born wrongs patiently? Have I forgiven injuries willingly? Do I pray for the living and the dead?

C. ASPECTS OF COMMUNAL ACTION

There are two kinds of apostolic groups: action groups and formation groups. The purpose of the first is simply to act apostolically. As examples of such groups we might mention the Confraternity of Christian Doctrine, interracial councils, and community development organizations. The purpose of the second is to *form* apostles, and here we might mention organizations such as the various third orders, the Christian Family Movement, and Young Christian Students.

Formation groups should be small, not much larger than the group of which Christ himself was the leader. Apostles cannot be produced *en masse*. The group must be small enough for each personality to emerge and develop within it. It must be small enough for the faith to be discussed in a very personal and familial manner.

The leadership in such groups should be as collegial as possible. This does not mean the absence of definite leadership. But it does mean that no one person should be allowed to control or dominate the group. In action groups this may at times be necessary. In formation groups it is invariably destructive. It inhibits the expression and development of all but one. Hence, in such groups the leader should seek to inspire rather than direct. He will try to create an atmosphere in which each member can feel free and responsible. He will inspire trust and encourage initiative, and rather than imposing his own personality and objectives upon the group, he will allow that personality and those objectives to emerge from the community itself.

As for the apostolic objectives of any group, they should always be concrete, practical, and possible. Men are most motivated by goals that are here and now attainable. If a group desires to operate within a frame of ultimate, long-range goals, this is fine and good, but these are no substitute for immediate objectives. A group without immediate realizable goals will never evoke the full-hearted commitment of all its members.

How are such objectives to be discovered? Cardinal Cardijn's formula is still the best available: observe, judge, act. *Observe:* study the situation, discover its needs, then select one of these needs for direct action. *Judge:* estimate what can be done here and now, analyze the best way to begin, map out a tentative plan. Then *Act:* act vigorously, communally, resourcefully, perseveringly. And retain flexibility. If one avenue closes, try another; if one field is found to be still not ripe for the harvest, try another. Do not get bogged down; be able to shift course quickly and decisively.

Most apostolic groups will want to have a priest chaplain. What is his role? With respect to the actions undertaken, his role should be supporting and subsidiary. His apostolic ministry is different from the ministry of laymen, and should remain so. With respect to the spiritual formation of the group, he has a leadership role but one in which he scrupulously avoids any attempt to dominate. His presence within the group (like Christ's presence with the Twelve) is the presence of a servant —a servant who enlightens, inspires, and unifies. Charity, trust, and deep respect should characterize his relation to the group, and its relation to him.

If we wish to acquire an apostolic outlook on life we need to understand ourselves as Christ understood himself—that is, first of all, as one *sent* by God, a missionary, a prophet; and secondly, as a *servant*, as one for whom to serve is to reign; and finally, as a *son*, and therefore as one who knows that his works and prayers have redemptive value in the sight of God. We are sent; we are servants; we are sons . . . which is another way of saying that we are prophets, kings, and priests.

Christ's death and resurrection was at once a prophetic, royal, and priestly act. It was prophetic inasmuch as it was a revelation of the depth of God's love for men. It was royal inasmuch as it was an event charged with power, power sufficient to overcome death itself, power to restore friendship between men and God. Lastly, it was a priestly act, a sacrifice, a holocaust in which Christ surrendered the totality of himself into the hands of his Father.

Earlier we said that Christ's life could not be partitioned into certain acts that were prophetic and others that were royal, but rather that these were two different dimensions of all of his activity. The same is true of his priestly ministry. Christ's whole life was priestly, just as his whole life was royal and prophetic. His whole life was sacrificial, just as his whole life bore witness to the truth and radiated divine power.

A sacrifice is not a bargain or a contract. There is nothing *quid pro quo* about it. If there were, it would be not a gift but a bribe. Generally a sacrifice is *anything done for God,* any expression of our love for him, any act inspired by that love. The more one man loves another the greater will be his desire to give him things. The same holds true of our relation with God. The more we love him the more will we want to give gifts to him—to offer sacrifice.

Seen thus, the act of sacrifice, although it may involve pain, is not of itself painful but rather joyful. It is an expression of love, and in such expressions man finds his fullest joy. To one who loves God deeply it would be painful not to offer sacrifice. It would be like not being able to communicate good news.

Strange to say, sacrifice has no effect upon God. Its effect is upon ourselves, not upon him. Normally, when we express our love to another person we "move" that person. In some way we alter their attitude, we brighten their day. But this is not true of our expressions of love toward God. His love for us is unalterable and unchangeable. Nothing we can do, however good or bad, can either diminish or enhance his uncreated love for us.

What, then, is the good of offering sacrifice? The good is *ours*. For in expressing our love for God we deepen and enrich it, we nourish and water it. Just as contrariwise, in not expressing that love we slowly cause it to wither and die. The same is true of the love between two people. When a boy stops seeing a girl, then stops telephoning her, then stops writing her, he soon stops thinking of her. His love slowly cools and disappears. It is not only our heart that influences our actions; our actions also influence our heart.

The fact that sacrifices do not "change" God's attitude toward us raises a question regarding so-called "sacrifices of petition"— offerings made in order to *get* as well as to *give*. For example, someone offers the Mass for the repose of the soul of a friend, or someone journeys to Lourdes in order to regain good health. True enough, these acts are sacrifices; but they are not only sacrifices. They are also prayers of petition. The offering is made to God out of love for him. It is a gift and therefore a sacrifice. Yet at the same time it is offered *for* men and out of love for them, and under this aspect it is a prayer of petition. Such was Christ's own sacrifice.

A sacrificial prayer of petition may, under divine providence, change the course of events; but this is not because it changes God's will but because it is itself part of God's plan for governing the world. Thus, when we say that Christ's sacrifice restored men to the love of God we do not mean that that sacrifice caused God to change his mind about men. No, for Christ's sacrifice was itself part of God's plan for men.

Paradoxically, it is ultimately God himself who offers every sacrifice. We see this clearly in the case of Christ. For the Father provided both the "matter" of his sacrifice (his humanity) and the "form" (he premoved and inspired Christ's will to offer it). The Father both initiated Christ's act of offering and provided the reality that was offered. The same is true of every sacrifice. Thus, every sacrifice begins and ends in God. In every sacrifice God is giving to God; God is loving God. Yet more: God is enabling men to share in his love for himself.

A. THE SACRIFICE OF CHRIST AND OF CHRISTIANS

If it is true that under the New Law there is only one sacrifice —that of Christ himself, is it correct for us to speak of acts like giving up cigarettes or saying the rosary as sacrifices?

Yes, these are true sacrifices, but only if two conditions are verified. First, they are sacrifices only if—implicitly or explicitly —they express the donation of one's whole self. For Christians there are no sacrifices but only self-sacrifices. Second, in order that the offering be integrated into Christ's offering, it is necessary that the offerer be incorporated into Christ's Mystical Body. Then such acts become "acceptable to God through Jesus Christ."

But what of someone who says he is giving up fornication or thievery? Can these be sacrifices? Obviously the sins themselves cannot be given to God, nor even the person's attachment to them. These would hardly be acceptable offerings. In these cases what one offers is the endurance and perseverance that such reforms entail. Properly speaking, we cannot even offer suffering to God, for suffering in and of itself is evil. Rather, we offer our acceptance of it and patience with it.

The English word "sacrifice" derives from two Latin words meaning "to make holy" (sacrum facere). This etymology can help us to remember that Christ's sacrifice was not complete until Easter Sunday, for only then was he wholly "sacrum," wholly transfused with divine glory and holiness.

Christ's sacrifice consisted in two movements: one of emptying and one of exaltation; one of death and one of resurrection. The same is true of every genuine Christian sacrifice. Each involves both a death and a resurrection. Each involves a conversion or transformation. This is begun with the "sacrifice" of Baptism when we die and rise with Christ, and it is perfected through every action in which we die to self and love for God. This sacrifice of the "self in Christ" will be consummated on the Last Day, when we will be wholly transfigured with divine life.

Only a free man (free in the Pauline sense) can offer sacrifice, for only a free man can give himself to God. Neither the devils nor those enslaved by them can surrender themselves to God. They are not spiritually free. On the other hand, those whom Christ has liberated have endless opportunities to offer sacrifice. Every one of their actions can be sacrificial.

Through their reception of the sacraments, through their acts of mortification and self-denial, through their works of charity, through their patience with the trials and sufferings of life, not only do they offer sacrifices but they also enlarge their freedom, and thus become ever more capable of giving themselves unreservedly to God. Seen from this angle, ascetic practices have the double value of not only being sacrifices but also of liberating us so as to make us more able to give ourselves to God.

Earlier we saw that the layman's share in Christ's priesthood issues from two sources: grace and the sacramental character. Grace makes us sons and thereby capacitates us to offer "spiritual sacrifices"; the character situates us in the Church and empowers us to take part in Christ's sacramental sacrifice. We shall now indicate some of the principal characteristics of spiritual sacrifice and some of the significant ways in which it can be offered. Then, we shall conclude by describing how the layman participates in the sacrifice of the Mass.

B. SPIRITUAL SACRIFICE

For an action to be a spiritual sacrifice it must have two characteristics. First, consciously or unconsciously, it must be done "in the Spirit"—that is, it must issue from a heart moved by the Holy Spirit. Otherwise it would not be united to Christ's sacrifice, for only the Holy Spirit can unite our works to his. Second, the action must be done *for God*.

This is not such a restricting qualification as might appear at first glance. For every human action is either selfish or unselfish, and if it is unselfish, it is ultimately directed to God. Too, Christ regards every gift given to our fellow man as a gift to himself. "Amen I say to you, as long as you did it for one of these, the least of my brethren, you did it for me" (Matt. 25:40).

Only selfish actions are positively excluded from being spiritual sacrifices, and even here we must not be too exclusive. Many actions done for self are not selfish and therefore can be sacrificial actions. For example, take something as seemingly "selfish" as eating. If one eats in order to live, and if one lives in order to serve others, then even one's eating acquires a sacrificial and redemptive dimension. Or, suppose a person, feeling unsociable, goes to his room some afternoon, closes the door, listens to a few tunes on the radio, enjoys a beer, and goes to sleep. If he does this to recoup his energies, the better to serve his neighbor on the morrow, this too is a spiritual sacrifice.[29]

Sacred Scripture singles out certain actions as particularly noteworthy spiritual sacrifices. Paul urged the Romans to worship God "by offering your living *bodies* as a holy sacrifice, truly pleasing to God" (Rom. 12:1; emphasis added). In Hebrews we read: "Through him (Christ), *let us offer God* an unending *sacrifice of praise,* a verbal sacrifice that is offered every time we acknowledge his name. Keep doing *good works* and *sharing your resources,* for these are sacrifices that please God" (Heb. 13:15–16; emphasis added). Other passages mention professing one's faith, almsgiving, works of mercy, and the preaching of the Gospel.

The Constitution on the Church provides a still more comprehensive listing. With reference to laymen the decree has this to say:

For all their works, prayers and apostolic endeavors, their ordinary married and family life, their daily occupations, their physical and mental relaxation, if carried out in the Spirit, and even the hardships of life, if patiently borne—all these become "spiritual sacrifices acceptable to God through Jesus Christ." [30]

Among the many ways in which Christians can offer such sacrifices, the following are particularly relevant for our day.

The sacrifice of time and energy. God has given each of us a limited span of time and a measured amount of energy. We are free to use them as we will, selfishly or unselfishly. We can dedicate them to the service of others or hoard them for the service of ourselves.

The man who has made this sacrifice has placed himself at the disposal of those whom he serves. He is available, accessible, approachable. Defining himself as a servant, he is fulfilled in giving service. He responds to people and to situations with his whole self, always ready to donate himself to others. He has taken to heart the words of Christ: "For anyone who wants to save his life will lose it; but anyone who loses his life for my sake, that man will save it" (Luke 9:24).

The sacrifice of autonomy. Men rightly prize their independence, and rightly will they sacrifice it only to what is greater—to other persons and to God. The sacrifice of one's autonomy involves obligating oneself to others; it involves assuming responsibilities. It entails binding one's own fate to the fate of another—to his weaknesses as well as to his strengths, to his failures as well as to his successes. It carries with it all the joys and all the sufferings of personal "coexistence." It commits one to bearing the burdens and sharing the sorrows of others. When lived to the full, it is a supreme expression of Christian love.

The sacrifice of service. Every human being is endowed with his own particular talents and abilities. One will be good at music, another will have a wonderful sense of humor, a third will have a keen mind, a fourth will have a strong and limber body, a fifth will have deep faith, a sixth will be naturally sympathetic and sensitive to others, a seventh will have a profound spirit of dedication. The list could go on and on. The Christian expresses his gratitude for the gifts that God has given him by placing them at the service of others. For example, the one who can sing will sing for others, and the one who can think will think for others, and the one who can hammer will hammer for others, and the one with the gift for prayer will pray for others.

Conscious that his gifts are from God and that God wills him to serve others through them, the Christian will earnestly strive to perfect the skills and abilities. The doctor will realize that the more he excels in his specialty the more perfectly will he be able to serve suffering men. And the housewife will know that her mastery of the art of homemaking will bring happiness and peace to all who dwell within. Thus, the very efforts we make to improve ourselves can be sacrifices, if only our self-improvement is directed to the service of others.

The sacrifice of security. Apostolic involvement always involves risks: the risk of rejection, the risk of failure, even sometimes the risk of life itself. Whenever we step out of the crowd, whenever we take Christian initiative, we become a potential target for others, or at least for their tongues. The love of being safe and secure, the desire not to expose oneself to criticism or danger of any kind, is perhaps the greatest internal enemy of the apostolate. Happily, however, courage inspires courage, and when one person breaks out of the vortex of fear that encases social life he makes it easier for the next. The Christian who sacrifices his security for the sake of the apostolate will usually soon find others at his side.

The sacrifice of attachment. Recent biblical studies have shown that Christ counseled *all* his followers to practice poverty, chastity, and obedience. Not that he asked all to take the vows of religious life but that he willed all to be poor in spirit, pure in heart, and obedient to the Word.

The layman practices *poverty* when charity governs his attitude toward material things, when he forfeits the superfluities of life that others might have the necessities, and when he uses his money not solely to satisfy himself but to do as much good for others as possible. He practices *chastity* when, through voluntary renunciation and mortification, he unchains himself from slavery to the flesh and when he sacrifices his own physical comfort for the spiritual and material well-being of others. He practices *obedience* by becoming ever more docile to the Word of God and ever more energetic in implementing it. The practice of these three counsels is an apostolic prerequisite. The man who is not detached from his possessions, his pleasures, and his own will cannot possess the zeal and spiritual sensitivity that should characterize the effective apostle.

The sacrifice of the cross. In Christian life the cross assumes many different modalities. To mention only a few: tiredness, sadness, anxiety, rejection, failure, loss of health, alienation, the catastrophes of life, and death itself. In all these ways men become victims. But none of it need be wasted. For if it is accepted and endured with Christian patience it becomes redemptive for ourselves and for others.

Suffering is tragic only when it becomes an occasion for man to curse his fate and the Maker of his fate. It is total loss only when one lets it break his faith and trust in God. It is gain whenever it is used as a springboard for acts of faith, hope, and charity. Death can be the greatest opportunity of all, occasioning a definitive and total act of self-surrender into the hands of God.

Although the Christian knows how to utilize the redemptive value of suffering, he looks at it with neither compliance nor delight. Christ's second great commandment—"You shall love your neighbor as yourself"—commits him to work for the minimization of his own and his neighbor's sufferings. He should therefore take the lead in exorcising the evils that have always punished men—poverty, hunger, disease, disasters of every sort. Yet he will still realize that no amount of human doing can ever completely banish suffering from the earth, and thus he is predisposed to accept the sufferings that cannot be here and now avoided and "make the most" of them. He does this by uniting them to the sufferings of Christ himself on Calvary, thus filling up in his own flesh what is lacking to the sufferings of Christ, for his body, which is the Church (Col. 1:24).

C. OFFERING THE SACRIFICE OF THE MASS

The Mass is a sacramental re-enactment of the selfsame sacrifice that Christ offered on Calvary. The same offering that was made on the first Good Friday is made again at Mass, "only the manner of offering is different." Why this perpetual renewal? For two principal reasons: first, that we might be continually reminded that *Christ is our sacrifice;* and second, that we might consciously and efficaciously *unite our self-offering to his.*

In Old Testament times men offered God their goats and rams, their sheep and the produce of their fields. These things served them as symbols for what they really meant to offer— namely, themselves. Now, Christ has become our goat, our ram. He has willed that we should "use" him as the expression of our love and worship of God. The unfailing acceptability of the Mass derives from just this: that Christ himself is our offering. And yet it is not sufficient simply to watch the Mass or simply to recall the event that it images. It avails us nothing unless we unite ourselves to it, unless "through him, with him, and in him" we use it to surrender the totality of our existence to the Father.

The various rites or rubrics of the Mass—the prayers, readings, music, symbolic actions—are all meant to engage our hearts and move us to deeper and deeper acts of self-donation. Together they are meant to make the Mass an event that will continually recharge our desire to be wholly conformed to God's will.

For this reason the Second Vatican Council enjoined a revision of the liturgy. The Council Fathers decreed that the new rites "should be distinguished by a noble simplicity; they should be short, clear, and unencumbered by useless repetition." [31] They should be "comprehensible to all," and hence largely in the language of those gathered around the altar. Ideally the liturgy should possess such vitality and beauty that it would quicken the spirits of all who take part in it. For when it is sluggish and boring, when it lacks grace and simplicity and intelligibility, far from generating devotion, it kills it.

The Mass is a communal celebration, a community work. Each offers for all, and all offer for each. The whole Mystical Body is involved—saints and sinners, the living and the dead, Africans, Asians, Europeans, Americans. We pray for the whole Church, but especially for those with whom God has situated us—our own particular Christian community. Where there is no sense of community, where parishioners do not feel interested in and responsible for one another, the Mass will not mean and effect all that it should.

How do Christians acquire this sense of community? Through active charity with and for each other, through a shared apostolate, through progressive leadership, and finally, through a living liturgy. The liturgy by itself will never create a true Christian community. It must be united to a vigorous communal apostolate.

But for the character imparted by Baptism, the layman could not operate sacramentally. The character enables him to offer Christ as his sacrifice, and to offer himself "in Christ." He does this by spiritually entering into the symbolic offering of bread and wine, and by concurring with the consecrating action of the ordained priest.

Only one who has received the sacrament of Orders can "confect" the sacrifice; only he (acting for Christ) can make Christ's sacrifice sacramentally present. But the layman, by wholeheartedly desiring and consenting to this action, "not only offers the sacrifice by the hands of the priest, but also, to a certain extent, in union with him." [32] Nor is this all. Being members of the Mystical Body, they can integrate their own self-offering into that of Christ. Thus the Mass becomes a sacrifice not only of the Head, but of the members as well. In so doing, the Christian truly *adds* to the Mass. His full participation makes it more sanctifying both for himself and for others than it would have been without it.

In the Mass we sacramentally express (and in expressing, intensify) our adherence to Christ and his people. We declare what we are and what we want to be. In eating the Lord's Supper together, we profess our unity with those with whom we share it and we affirm our intention to live with them as brothers. If these declarations are not to be void, our whole life should bespeak them so that we become living expressions, living witnesses, of Christian love.

For the fully committed Christian the Mass will be both the source and the summit of his life. It will be the *summit* inasmuch as it is the culminating expression of his Christian identity. There, more than anywhere else, he enters into the life to which he is eternally called—a life of communion with Christ and all men in Christ. It will be the *source* inasmuch as at Mass he rededicates his spirit to the work of establishing Christ's kingdom—a kingdom of truth, justice, love, and freedom. Such a Christian brings his life into the Mass, and the Mass into his life.

NOTES

1. Yves Congar, O.P., *Lay People in the Church,* p. 114.
2. Roland de Vaux, O.P., *Ancient Israel: Its Life and Institutions,* p. 356.
3. Augustine, *The City of God,* 10, 6.
4. John Damascene, *De fide orthodoxa,* 3, 3, PG 94, 989b.
5. C. V. Héris, O.P., *The Mystery of Christ,* p. 70.
6. Jerome, *In Isaiam,* 61, 1. PL 24, 599.
7. Peter Damien, *Opuscula,* 6, 4. PL 145, 103.
8. I. De la Potterie, S.J., "L'Onction du Christ," *Nouvelle Revue Théologique,* 80 (1958), 238.
9. Joseph Lecuyer, *Le Sacerdoce dans le mystère du Christ,* p. 110.
10. Council of Trent (Session 22, A.D. 1562), *Teaching on the Most Holy Sacrifice of the Mass,* 1.
11. Christopher Kiesling, O.P., *The Spirit and Practice of the Liturgy,* p. 33.
12. Gregory the Great, *Moralium,* I, xiv, 32. PL 75, 542.
13. T. F. Torrance, *Royal Priesthood,* p. 37.
14. Herbert McCabe, O.P., *The People of God,* p. 38.
15. John Chrysostom, *In Matthaeum homiliae,* 82, 5. PG 60, 743.
16. Ernst Mura, *The Nature of the Mystical Body,* p. 119.
17. Henri de Lubac, S.J., *The Splendour of the Church,* p. 129.
18. Ceslaus Spicq, O.P., *L'Epître aux Hébreux,* II, 94.
19. Justin Martyr, *Dialogue with Trypho.* PG 6, 744–745.
20. Irenaeus, *Adversus haereses,* 4. PG 7, 995.
21. Origen, *In Leviticam homilium,* GCS 29, 436.

22. John Chrysostom, *On the Second Epistle to the Corinthians.* PG 61, 417–418.

23. Augustine, *Sermo* 48, II, 2. PL 38, 317.

24. Cited in Cyril Eastwood, *The Priesthood of All Believers,* p. 115.

25. *Catechism of the Council of Trent,* II, 7, q. 23.

26. J. Lindblom, *Prophecy in Ancient Israel,* p. 1.

27. I. Montuclard, *Les événements et la foi,* p. 61. See Léon Joseph Suenens, *The Gospel to Every Creature,* p. 18.

28. Augustine, *Sermo* 340, 1. PL 38, 1483.

29. This is not to imply that there is anything indecent about enjoying a good meal or a good tune or a good sleep that is not consciously referred to one's apostolic life. These are all gifts from the Creator and were meant to be enjoyed. The secret is "to care and not to care," in the words of Gerald Vann. For a balanced perspective on the value of sense experiences, see C.-D. Boulogne, O.P., *My Friends the Senses* (New York, Kenedy, 1953). See also the passage on leisure, pp. 117 f. of our book.

30. Paul VI, *Constitution on the Church,* 34.

31. *Ibid.*

32. Pius XII, *Mediator Dei,* 92.

BIBLIOGRAPHY

Note: When a foreign-language work now available in English translation is entered first under its original title, the original edition, and not the English, was consulted by the author. The English title has been supplied for the reader's information.

Audet, L. "Notre participation au sacerdoce du Christ," *Laval Théologique et Philosophique*, 1 (1945), 9–46, 257–301.

Barden, W., O.P. *What Happens at Mass.* Staten Island (N.Y.), Alba House, 1963.

Benoit, P., O.P., and others. *The Eucharist in the New Testament.* Trans. by E. M. Steward. Baltimore, Helicon, 1964.

Buttrick, G. A. (ed.). *The Interpreter's Dictionary of the Bible.* 4 vols. Nashville, Abingdon, 1962.

Congar, Y., O.P. *Lay People in the Church.* Trans. by D. Attwater. Westminster (Md.), Newman, 1956.

Cox, H. *The Secular City.* New York, Macmillan, 1965.

Cunningham, F., O.P. *The Indwelling of the Trinity.* Dubuque, Priory, 1955.

Dabin, P., S.J. *Le Sacerdoce royal des fidèles.* Paris, Desclée, 1950.

Davis, C. *Sacraments of Initiation.* New York, Sheed & Ward, 1965.

Dillenschneider, C., C.Ss.R. *Le Christ, L'unique prêtre, et nous ses prêtres.* 2 vols. Paris, Alsatia, 1959. English ed.: *Christ the One Priest and We His Priests.* Trans. by S. M. Renelle, S.S.N.D. St. Louis, Herder, 1965.

Durrwell, F. X., C.Ss.R. *The Resurrection*. Trans. by R. Sheed. New York, Sheed & Ward, 1960.

Eastwood, C. *The Priesthood of All Believers*. Minneapolis, Augsburg, 1960.

Fransen, P., S.J. *Divine Grace and Man*. Trans. by G. Dupont, S.J. New York, New American Library, 1965.

Hamer, J., O.P. *The Church Is a Communion*. Trans. by G. Chapman. New York, Sheed & Ward, 1964.

Herbert, A. S. *Worship in Ancient Israel*. Richmond, John Knox, 1959.

Héris, C. V., O.P. *The Mystery of Christ*. Trans. by D. Fahey, C.S.Sp. Westminster (Md.), Newman, 1950.

John XXIII. *Mater et Magistra*. NCWC trans. Washington, NCWC, 1961.

————. *Pacem in Terris*. NCWC trans. *Ibid.*, 1963.

Journet, C. *L'Église du Verbe incarné*. Bruges, Desclée, 1941. English ed.: *The Church of the Word Incarnate*. Trans. by A. H. C. Downes. New York, Sheed & Ward, 1955.

Kiesling, C., O.P. "The Sacramental Character and the Liturgy," *The Thomist*, 27 (1963), 385–412.

————. *The Spirit and Practice of the Liturgy*. Chicago, Priory, 1965.

Kraemer, H. *A Theology of the Laity*. Philadelphia, Westminster, 1958.

La Potterie, I. de, S.J. "L'Onction du Christ," *Nouvelle Revue Théologique*, 80 (1958), 225–252.

La Taille, M. de, S.J. *The Mystery of Faith*. Trans. in part by J. B. Schimpf. 2 vols. New York, Sheed & Ward, 1940.

Lecuyer, J. *Le Sacerdoce dans le mystère du Christ*. Paris, Cerf, 1957.

Leeming, B., S.J. *Principles of Sacramental Theology*. Westminster (Md.), Newman, 1956.

Lindblom, J. *Prophecy in Ancient Israel*. Philadelphia, Fortress, 1962.

Lubac, H. de, S.J. *The Splendour of the Church*. Trans. M. Mason. New York, Sheed & Ward, 1955.

McCabe, H., O.P. *The People of God.* New York, Sheed & Ward, 1964.

McNamara, K. "Aspects of the Layman's Role in the Mystical Body," *Irish Theological Quarterly,* 25 (1963), 124–143.

Mura, E., C.F.V. *The Nature of the Mystical Body.* Trans. by A. Bouchard. New York, Herder & Herder, 1963.

O'Neill, C., O.P. "The Instrumentality of the Sacramental Character," *Irish Theological Quarterly,* 25 (1963), 262–268.

———. *Meeting Christ in the Sacraments.* Staten Island (N.Y.), Alba House, 1963.

———. "The Role of the Recipient and Sacramental Signification," *The Thomist,* 21 (1958), 257–301, 508–540.

Paul VI. *Constitution on the Church.* NCWC trans. Washington, NCWC, 1964.

———. *Constitution on the Liturgy.* NCWC trans. *Ibid.,* 1963.

———. *Decree on the Apostolate of the Laity.* NCWC trans. *Ibid.,* 1965.

Pius XII. *Mediator Dei.* NCWC trans. Washington, NCWC, 1948.

———. *Mystici Corporis.* NCWC trans. *Ibid.,* 1943.

Rahner, K., S.J. *The Christian Commitment.* Trans. by C. Hastings. New York, Sheed & Ward, 1963.

———. *The Church and the Sacraments.* Trans. by W. J. O'Hara. New York, Herder & Herder, 1964.

———. "The Lay Apostolate" (trans. by J. Hess), *Cross Currents,* 7 (1957), 225–246.

———. *The Theology of Death.* Trans. by C. Henkey. New York, Herder & Herder, 1961.

Rea, J. E. *The Common Priesthood of the Members of the Mystical Body.* Westminster (Md.), Newman, 1947.

Ringgren, H. *Sacrifice in the Bible.* New York, Association, 1962.

Robinson, J. *The New Reformation.* Philadelphia, Westminster, 1965.

Ryan, L. "Vatican II and the Priesthood of the Laity," *Irish Theological Quarterly,* 32 (1965), 93–116.

Schillebeeckx, E., O.P. *Christ the Sacrament of the Encounter with God.* Trans. by P. Barrett; rev. by M. Schoof and L. Bright. New York, Sheed & Ward, 1963.

Schroeder, H. J., O.P. *Canons and Decrees of the Council of Trent.* St. Louis, Herder, 1941.

Spicq, C., O.P. *L'Epître aux Hébreux.* 2 vols. Paris, Gabalda, 1952.

Suenens, L. J. *The Gospel to Every Creature.* Westminster (Md.), Newman, 1965.

Suhard, E. *The Church Today: The Collected Writings of Emmanuel Cardinal Suhard.* Ed. by L. J. Putz and V. J. Giese. Chicago, Fides, 1953.

Teilhard de Chardin, P., S.J. *The Divine Milieu.* Trans. by B. Wall. New York, Harper & Row, 1960.

Thurian, M. *The Eucharistic Memorial.* Trans. by J. G. Davies (Part 1). Richmond, John Knox, 1960.

Torrance, T. F. *Royal Priesthood.* London, Oliver & Boyd, 1955.

Vaux, R. de, O.P. *Ancient Israel: Its Life and Institutions.* Trans. by J. McHugh. New York, McGraw-Hill, 1961.

Visser't Hooft, W. A. *The Pressure of Our Common Calling.* Garden City (N.Y.), Doubleday, 1959.

Westcott, B. F. *The Epistle to the Hebrews.* Grand Rapids, Eerdmans, 1892.

Yerkes, R. K. *Sacrifice in Greek and Roman Religions and Early Judaism.* New York, Scribner, 1952.